Exiles from Eden

EXILES FROM EDEN

Religion and the
Academic Vocation in America

MARK R. SCHWEHN

New York   Oxford
OXFORD UNIVERSITY PRESS
1993

Oxford University Press

Oxford   New York   Toronto
Delhi   Bombay   Calcutta   Madras   Karachi
Kuala Lumpur   Singapore   Hong Kong   Tokyo
Nairobi   Dar es Salaam   Cape Town
Melbourne   Auckland   Madrid

and associated companies in
Berlin   Ibadan

Copyright © 1993 by Mark R. Schwehn

Published by Oxford University Press, Inc.

198 Madison Avenue, New York, New York 10016-4314

Oxford is a registered trademark of Oxford University Press, Inc.

Library of Congress Cataloging-in-Publication Data
Schwehn, Mark R., 1945–
Exiles from Eden : religion and the academic vocation in America /
Mark R. Schwehn.   p. cm.   Includes index.
ISBN 0-19-507343-6
1. College teachers—United States—Intellectual life.
2. Universities and colleges—United States—Religion. 3. College
teaching—United States—Philosophy. 4. Education, Higher—United
States—Aims and objectives. I. Title.
LB1778.2.S38 1993 378.1'2—dc20   92–13951

4 6 8 9 7 5

Printed in the United States of America
on acid-free paper

For
Kaethe, Martha, and John
To
Dorothy

PREFACE

On a spring evening in 1982, I sat in a circle of my colleagues from the University of Chicago and from other institutions of higher learning in the Chicago area. We were meeting together as the Chicago Group on the History of the Social Sciences, convened by Professor George Stocking of the Anthropology Department. We had all read a paper prepared by one of the members of the group, and roughly eight of the twelve or so of us had arrived to discuss it. The paper, like most of those presented to the group, examined some aspect of the professionalization of the social sciences. I remember little else about the setting that evening, except that I was sitting directly to the right of Professor Stocking.

While we were waiting for the remainder of the expected participants to straggle into our midst, someone (I think it was Peter Novick but I cannot be sure) made the following proposal: "We've just recently filed our income tax forms; let's move around the circle from left to right and indicate what each of us wrote under the heading 'occupation.'" This simple exercise was thought to have potentially profound and self-revealing implications. And so it proved.

The first person spoke up at once with a kind of brisk confidence. "Sociologist," he said. And so it continued—"anthropologist," "historian," "psychologist," "historian." At about this point (though I have sometimes been slow to catch the drift of things, I did discern this time a clear pattern emerging), I began to wonder whether or not I had the courage to be honest in the company of so many of my senior colleagues.

Though trained as an intellectual historian, I had never once thought to put such a designation down under "occupation" on my tax form. When I finally spoke up, I admitted (it certainly felt like an admission) that I had written "college teacher" under the relevant heading. This disclosure was greeted with what I can only describe (though it was doubtless a projection even then) as a combination of mild alarm and studied astonishment. I felt as though I had suddenly become, however briefly, an informant from another culture.

This experience and others like it at the University of Chicago led me to explore, over the course of the last decade, the meaning of the academic vocation in the United States. This exploration entailed two related tasks. First, I tried to discover what the academic vocation had become by examining contemporary academic practices, by learning about the history of higher education in this country, and by studying some of the important formulations of the academic calling that have been offered over the course of the last century. Second, I sought to reflect critically upon what the academic vocation had come to mean for me.

The present book accordingly begins by unpacking one commonplace of academic life—the mysterious complaint, "I don't have enough time to *do my own work*"—and by engaging one of the most closely argued and most culturally influential accounts of the academic calling ever written, Max Weber's "Academics as a Vocation." My study of Weber's account of the academic calling led me to investigate the larger subject of this book, the relationship between religion and higher learning. The logic of the problem of vocation impelled me in this direction, because Weber, in the course of his statement of the academic calling, self-consciously transmuted a number of terms and ideas that were religious in origin and implication. Even so, my interest in the relationship between religion and higher learning was and remains really more of a chronological matter than a strictly logical one. Indeed, the title of this book, *Exiles from Eden: Religion and the Academic Vocation in America*, is, as they say, another story.

Later in 1982 I resigned my position at the University of Chicago, after eight years of teaching there, and I accepted an appointment in the honors college of Valparaiso University. I did this for several reasons, but perhaps the main one of them was that I found that I could pursue my own sense of the academic vocation more fully and responsibly at Valparaiso than I could at Chicago. Valparaiso is a church-related university, and Chicago is not. Valparaiso therefore strives to keep certain questions alive, such as questions about the relationship between religious faith and the pursuit of truth, that were then and still are close to the center of my understanding of the meaning of academic life. In brief,

I sought to think through the problem of the academic vocation in part by living through it.

In the same year that I arrived at Valparaiso University, Clifford Geertz published a stimulating collection of essays entitled *Local Knowledge: Further Essays in Interpretive Anthropology.* In the midst of one of the essays, he remarked upon a career pattern peculiar to academics, "namely, that one starts at the center of things and then moves toward the edges." Most academics, he noted, begin their careers at one or another of the great research universities and then proceed directly to schools that are "lower down or further out—whatever the image should be." Given my own experience at the time I read the essay, I was most forcefully struck by Geertz's figuration of the mentality that accompanies this pattern. He called it the "exile from Eden syndrome."[1]

Nothing in my own or in my religious tradition's reading of the great creation narratives in Genesis 1–3 had prepared me to consider the University of Chicago as Eden. Indeed, I thought I had good reason to suspect that places like the university were nurseries of the very temptations that had led to Eden's demise. Chicago had seemed to me in some respects like an alluring image of paradise lost. The relatively small university in the midst of northwest Indiana's snow belt to which I had gone was far from perfect by Chicago's exacting standards of excellence, but *Valparaiso* at least meant "vale of paradise." At any rate, Geertz, a self-proclaimed disciple of Weber, seemed to be thinking about the modern academy in terms that were, like Weber's own, borrowed from a religious vocabulary whose meanings had been strangely inverted. Viewing my own story through Weberian eyes, I had come to see how deep were the tensions between my own understanding of my calling and the modern university's understanding of it.

This book is the outcome of those tensions, but it is not a record of them. I think it only fair to alert the reader, through these brief stories, to the personal investment I have in the subject of this book. But I do not intend here an *apologia pro vita sua.* I simply do not have a life that would warrant an undertaking of that kind, as any comparison between my *vita* and Cardinal Newman's would conclusively demonstrate.

Nor is this book an effort to vindicate the value of church-related institutions of higher learning at the expense of secular colleges and universities. I owe a large part of whatever intellectual merit this book has to the education I received at Stanford and Chicago. I came *to* Valparaiso; I did not really leave Chicago. On the other hand, I believe that all three of the institutions I have just mentioned need to reassess the meaning and the purpose of academic life. This book is intended as a contribution to that process of reappraisal, a process that must continue indefinitely within a pluralistic context. My intended audience therefore includes all of those who care about higher education in America today: faculty, students, administrators, trustees, foundation officers, and, beyond them, that large segment of the educated American public that worries over the future of higher education in this country.

The argument of the book will develop in the following manner. The first chapter offers an analysis and a critique of present-day conceptions of the academic vocation. The second chapter argues that one of the main currents in contemporary thought, the resurgence of conversation about community, warrants a religiously informed reconception of the academic vocation in particular and of academic life in general. The third chapter develops such a redescription, and the fourth attempts to answer certain objections that might be raised against it. In the last chapter, I try both to sum up and to extend my discussion of religion and higher learning by engaging the classic literary exploration of these subjects by an American modernist, *The Education of Henry Adams*. As Weber transmuted a religious tradition in the course of formulating the modern conception of the academic vocation, so Adams transmuted a religious myth of creation in the course of formulating his account of the modern educated personality.

Like most books, this one developed in part through a process of restricting the scope of the author's original ambitions. I had once hoped to locate my discussion of religion and higher learning within a multicultural context. I can now only confess my relative ignorance of the great religions of the world with the exception of Christianity. I have learned just enough about other religious traditions to be consistently modest about most of my claims. So, for example, when I write about certain Christian virtues and affections such as humility, piety, and charity, I do not mean to claim that these virtues are *distinctively* Christian. And when I claim that such virtues *are* religious, I mean this in the strictly historical sense that they arose originally within communities that were self-consciously religious in character. I do not mean thereby to suggest that only theists can be humble and charitable.

People from all religious backgrounds have chosen, over the course of the last century, to leave the "Edens" of academe and to pursue their own sense of academic vocation as exiles "on the periphery." I have learned from the examples of some of these people, such as Henry David Aiken, whose pilgrimage from Harvard to Brandeis in the mid-1960s inspired his provocative analysis of the modern academy in the *Predicament of the University*. As a Christian, I can only affirm, as one of the basic attitudes that informs this book, what Aiken describes as his own "hard-won achievement as a Jew." With him, I believe that "any authentic affirmation of one's humanity begins at home, moving out toward others in the form of a large-spirited hospitality which, in offering refuge or possible friendship to the stranger, can respect his inviolate being only if one honors one's own." [2]

Following Aiken's lead, I shall write in this book from a perspective informed by the Christian tradition but hospitable to other religious people and to secularists as well. Toward Aiken and others like him, I avow a sense of spiritual kinship. Toward Geertz and other self-styled denizens of the "Edens" of academe, I must avow the status of a self-imposed exile and strive for the kind of insight that is uniquely available to some of these persons. To all readers, I avow my own doubts about both the propriety and the usefulness of Edenic and exilic imagery to distinguish distinct places or groups *within* the present-day academy. Perhaps the place to begin an inquiry into the nature of the academic vocation is with the acknowledgment that we are all exiles from Eden.

Notes

1. "The Way We Think Now: Toward an Ethnography of Modern Thought," in Clifford Geertz, *Local Knowledge: Further Essays in Interpretive Anthropology* (Basic Books: New York, 1983), 158–59.
2. Henry David Aiken, *Predicament of the University* (Indiana University Press: Bloomington and London, 1971), 60.

Valparaiso, Indiana　　　　　　　　　　　　　　　　　　　M. S.
April 1992

ACKNOWLEDGMENTS

I want first to acknowledge the many excellent teachers who formed the character of my thinking through the years: in my undergraduate days at Valparaiso University, Will Boyd, Ken Klein, and Richard Baepler; in graduate school at Stanford, Allan Matusow and David Kennedy; subsequently, at the University of Chicago, Leon and Amy Kass, who made excellence in teaching visible by their examples.

Many friends and colleagues read portions of this book and by their responses strengthened its argument: Tom Kennedy, Renu Juneja, James Chandler, Gail Eifrig, Seymour Moskowitz, Arlin Meyer, Jon Pahl, David Rowland, Richard Wood, Douglas Sloan, Harry Liebersohn, Joe Hough, Jeff Smith, Joe Hensick, Parker Palmer, and John Feaster. I owe a special debt of gratitude to those who read the entire manuscript and who offered detailed criticisms: Fredrick Barton, Gilbert Meilaender, David Morgan, and Craig Dykstra; James Nuechterlein, who published portions of it in *The Cresset* and *First Things;* and the Christ College faculty—Michael Caldwell, Paul J. Contino, Clare Pearson Geiman, William Olmsted, John Steven Paul, Mel Piehl, and Warren Rubel. Cynthia Read, my editor at Oxford, made several pointed suggestions, all of which improved the quality of the book. Robert Wood Lynn supported my work on this project from beginning to end, combining for me, as he has for many others, the rigors of collaborative work with the pleasures of friendship.

The Valparaiso University School of Law made it possible for me to write this book in an atmosphere of ease and opulence. I owe special thanks to Ivan Bodensteiner, Bruce Berner, Alfred Meyer, Mary Moore, and Pat McRae for making the arrangements and providing the support that made me feel so much at home there. Elene Amundsen and Margaret Franson in the Christ College Dean's office helped me in more ways than I can enumerate here. The entire project was funded by a generous grant from the Lilly Endowment.

I am grateful to the following for permission to reprint copyright material in this book: the editor of *The Cresset* for "Making Sense of College Students," (November 1983): 11–14; "Academics as a Vocation," (April 1985): 4–9; and "Academics as a Vocation II," (May 1985): 5–10; and to the editor of *First Things: A Monthly Journal of Religion and Public Life* for "Religion and the Life of Learning," (August–September 1990): 34–43.

Finally, without the love of those to whom this book is dedicated and for whom this book is written, I might have lost heart. Their gifts to me are far beyond friendship, even beyond words.

CONTENTS

Exiles from Eden

1

The Academic Vocation

I

In this chapter, I shall try to advance our thinking about college and university education in the United States through a critical study of contemporary conceptions of the academic vocation. Current reflection upon the state of higher learning in America makes this task at once more urgent and more difficult than it has ever been since the rise of the modern research university. Consider, for example, former Harvard President Derek Bok's 1986–87 report to the Harvard Board of Overseers. On the one hand, Bok repeatedly insists that universities are obliged to help students learn how to lead ethical, fulfilling lives. On the other hand, he admits that faculty are ill-equipped to help the university discharge this obligation. "Professors," Bok writes, ". . . are trained to transmit knowledge and skills within their chosen discipline, not to help students become more mature, morally perceptive human beings."[1]

Notice Bok's assumptions. Teaching history or chemistry or mathematics or literature has little or nothing to do with forming students' characters. Faculty members must therefore be exhorted, cajoled, or otherwise maneuvered to undertake this latter endeavor *in addition to* teaching their chosen disciplines. The pursuit of knowledge and the cultivation of virtue are, for Bok at least, utterly discrete activities. To complicate matters still further, the Harvard faculty, together with most faculty members at other modern research universities, would very probably resist the notion that their principal vocational obligation is, as

Bok suggested, to transmit the knowledge and skills of their disciplines. They believe that their calling *primarily* involves *making* or advancing knowledge, not transmitting it.

How else could we explain the familiar academic lament "Because this is a terribly busy semester for me, I do not have any time to do my own work"? Among all occupational groups other than the professoriate, such a complaint, voiced under conditions of intensive labor, is inconceivable. Among university faculty members, it is *expected*. Never mind the number of classes taught, courses prepared, papers graded, and committees convened. Indeed, the more these activities increase, the more deeply the depressing conviction sets in: "I'M NOT DOING ENOUGH OF MY OWN WORK."

One is tempted to ask, Well then, whose work are you doing? To which question the response would be instantly forthcoming: You know what I mean; I'm not getting enough writing/composing/experimenting done. Though this response *seems* to clear up a certain amount of conceptual confusion, it does so by evading the depth grammar of the original remark. Faculty members, in the present case, *do* say what they mean: they believe that their own work *just is* writing, composing, and experimenting.

In what follows, I shall not attempt to set before the reader various alternative understandings of the academic vocation and then to argue for a preferred version. Indeed, an ethnography of academia in the United States today would probably reveal that, in operational terms at least, the work of university faculty members is defined by all three of the objectives adumbrated above—making knowledge, transmitting knowledge and skills, and helping students learn how to lead more ethical, fulfilling lives. Yet even though these three objectives do not seem inherently competing, much less contradictory, academicians have come to think of them in these terms. Thus, Bok appears to have thought that transmitting knowledge and skills is not relevant to character formation, and many faculty believe that, though they are expected somehow to pursue many objectives, their own work should be evaluated primarily, perhaps exclusively, in terms of one of them.

Such apparently widespread uncertainty about the purposes of higher learning in the United States has occasioned my inquiry here. My topic is just this uncertainty construed as a vocational problem. I shall endeavor first to show how this vocational problem arose, second to consider its epistemological aspects, and third to explore its religious dimensions. My thesis is that matters are more complex than Bok suggests. Current conceptions of the academic vocation actually militate against the pursuit of the project he once set before his own university.

II

Why do so many academics labor with an unsettled conscience? A preliminary answer to this question is not far to seek. The fact that university faculty tend to think that classroom teaching and collegiality are strangely *not* part of their "own work" is a tribute to the socializing power of our graduate schools. There students learn, regardless of their field of study, that research and publication constitute their tasks and that all other activities—teaching, lecturing, university service—somehow just go with the territory. The feeble efforts that most graduate schools make to provide their students with "teaching experience" (it is rather like giving would-be doctors training in "bedside manner": the training seems vaguely distasteful, but it somehow must be done) merely reinforces the suspicion that pedagogy is really not a part of one's work. Leaving aside the very important question of whether or not any teacher-training program could be successful at the graduate level (Tell me, Socrates, can teaching be taught?), the results of five to ten years of graduate training are unmistakable. Publication, graduate students discover, is *the* vocational aspiration. To expect a recent Ph.D. to think otherwise would be the same as expecting a recent law school graduate to think like an engineer.

This socializing process leads to what is perhaps the major "internal contradiction" within the enterprise of higher learning, because the vast majority of those Ph.D.'s who remain within the academy publish very little. Instead, "their own work" really consists of transmitting knowledge and skills and perhaps helping students to learn how to lead more ethical, fulfilling lives. Moreover, we have many institutions of higher learning in this country that explicitly emphasize and reward such endeavors as much as, in a few cases more than, published research.

The "internal contradiction" remains, however (a plurality of academies dedicated to distinctive aims does not resolve the contradiction), for three reasons. First, faculty at all colleges and universities are trained and socialized at modern research universities where the supreme value of making and advancing knowledge is deeply instilled within them.

Second, lateral or "upward" mobility from one institution to another depends primarily upon research and publication. Finally, aspirations to higher levels of excellence among the vast majority of colleges and universities of all types are invariably linked to publication and research, that is, to becoming more like Harvard, Yale, Stanford, and Chicago. In brief, we might have a variety of conceptions of the academic vocation both in theory and in practice, but one conception—that of the academic as one who makes knowledge—has long since attained hegemony over all the others.

This predominance was, moreover, achieved in the course of struggles against both the conception of the academic vocation that emphasized the transmission of knowledge and skills and the conception of the academic vocation that emphasized the cultivation of character. These conflicts, though they emerged everywhere in the Western world during the late nineteenth and early twentieth centuries, were most pronounced and dramatic in Germany. By comparison to their counterparts in the United States, France, and even England during this period, the German professoriate commanded an inordinately large amount of social prestige and influence. Thus, rival conceptions of the academic vocation were more sharply drawn and more culturally momentous there than elsewhere. Thus too, Max Weber's famous address, delivered at the end of this period at Munich University in 1918 and entitled "Wissenschaft als Beruf," remains even today the *locus classicus* for the elucidation of what has become the predominant understanding of the academic calling.[2]

Abandoning his ordinarily dry and measured style as the occasion moved him to do so, Weber issued a series of impassioned and uncompromising statements about the character of the academic calling.

> Whoever lacks the capacity to put on blinders, so to speak, and to come up to the idea that the *fate of his soul* depends upon whether or not he makes the correct conjecture at this passage of his manuscript may as well stay away from academics. He will never have what one may call the "personal experience" of academics. Without this strange intoxication, ridiculed by every outsider; without this passion, this "thousands of years must pass before you enter into life and thousands more wait in silence"—according to whether or not you succeed in making this conjecture; without this, you have *no* calling for academics and you should do something else.[3]

Remarks such as these were addressed to two audiences, one of them immediate, the other implied. The immediate audience consisted of many German students who were demanding that their teachers should become seers and prophets, asking professors to assume roles they could not responsibly perform. Some of these students were also seeking to forego the rigors of disciplined learning and to pursue instead a cult of immediate experience. In refusing the role of prophet, and in defending methodical intellectual procedures, Weber was reaffirming what he took to be the great legacy of the Enlightenment against the perilous irrationality of his contemporaries.

Weber's implied audience consisted of the guardians of what Fritz Ringer has called the German mandarin tradition of learning. This tradition, whose tenets virtually defined the shape and the substance of higher learning in Germany during the nineteenth century, had emphasized the cultivation of the mind and the spirit (*Bildung*), in other words the formation of character, as the supreme end of education. Those called to academics were, according to the mandarins, obliged to select those materials that would, through proper pedagogy, form the souls of students in accordance with certain classical notions of wisdom and virtue.[4] Accordingly, for a mandarin like Karl Jaspers, scholarship, however specialized, had a spiritual aspect insofar as it "does not forget the end for the means, does not become emerged in mere details, and does not lose . . . the idea of universitas."[5] Education, as opposed to instruction, involved "forming of the personality in accordance with an ideal of *Bildung* with ethical norms. . . . Education is the inclusive, the whole."[6]

Weber relentlessly attacked such elevated notions of the academic vocation. He insisted that separate departments of learning were finally so many warring gods, self-sufficient spheres in permanent and irreconcilable collision, not parts of some larger whole. Academics were, therefore, true to their own calling when they steadfastly refused to address questions about the meaning of the whole or the purpose of human life. Under such circumstances academic life could no longer be understood as "the way to true being, the way to true art, the way to true God, or the way to true happiness."[7]

The relevance of formulations such as these to the present academic experience in the United States is everywhere apparent, but it is nonetheless very difficult to explain. Weber began "Wissenschaft als Beruf" by stressing the *difference* between the social and material conditions of higher learning in the United States and Germany. And indeed the founders of the modern research university in this country consistently discovered that German models, however attractive they seemed in theory, were not readily adaptable in practice. From the 1860s through World War I and beyond, leading educators in this country stressed the importance of good teaching as a way of transmitting a tradition of liberal learning as much as they celebrated the importance of specialized, original, and published research.[8]

Yet even though the hegemony of the Weberian conception of the academic calling arrived later here than in Germany, mainly because of the comparatively pluralistic and decentralized character of higher learning in the United States, our own history is marked by debates that were very similar to those within Germany. Thus, for example, Hofstadter and Metzger characterize the rise of the university in this country as a movement "from inculcation to inquiry," from the transmission of knowledge and tradition to research.[9] Thus too, the formation versus information debates that occupied Harvard in the 1870s and 1880s were framed in terms that were remarkably similar to Jaspers's distinction between education (*Erziehung*), which involved *Bildung,* and instruction (*Unterricht*), which "merely" involved imparting of information and skills.[10] Finally and quite recently, Derek Bok could assume without question that teaching and research have little or nothing to do with character formation. He therefore proceeded to argue that Harvard should dedicate itself (a better sense of history would have led him to say that it should rededicate itself) to helping students lead more ethical and fulfilling lives in the face of a faculty not at all prepared to undertake this task.

On the basis of this cursory historical review, one might well be tempted to suppose that the rise of the modern research university and the concurrent ascendancy of the Weberian notion of the academic calling entailed only a "rearrangement of priorities" within the general field of higher learning in America. Yes, scholarship has been promoted in importance, and transmission of knowledge and skills, as well as character formation, have been demoted, but all three remain, in fact and in theory, purposes that inform current conceptions of the academic vocation. Some such account as this is the conventional view of matters.

The view turns out to be largely mistaken, however, for reasons that Weber himself acknowledged. He realized that by promoting original scholarship to the position of "our own work," he was advancing an account of the academic calling that was inimical to the kind of character formation associated with *Bildung*. And if Weber was correct on this point, as I believe that he was, it would be more accurate to claim that Harvard University has in part caused the problems that Bok and others have so recently discovered, that the modern university in its present form militates against some of the very purposes that it occasionally espouses. To see how and why this is so, I should like to turn to Weber once again, this time with special attention to the epistemic context of his account of the academic calling.

III

Weber elaborated his stringent conception of the academic calling first by locating it within the context of modernity and then by connecting it to the character of academic knowledge. "The fate of our times," he wrote, "is characterized by rationalization and intellectualization and, above all, by the *disenchantment of the world*. Precisely the ultimate and most sublime values have retreated from public life either into the transcendental realm of mystical life or into the brotherliness of direct and personal human relations."[11] Academic life was, for Weber, both the result and a cause of this ever-accelerating process of disenchantment that had been going on for thousands of years.

In practical terms this process of rationalization meant that we could "in principle master all things by calculation."[12] The end of academic life was nothing less than mastery of the world. In order to secure such mastery, academics had to work to extend the frontiers of learning within their own separate specialties. Indeed, academic work was forever "chained to the course of progress."[13] Academics could not work without at the same time hoping that their work would be surpassed ad infinitum. Publishing could thus have no meaning apart from the larger process of intellectualization that it furthered, and this process gave to the academic calling the only meaning that it could reasonably have in the world of modernity.

The character of academic inquiry implied by the term *rationalization* was, for Weber, purely formal, and the character of academic knowledge was purely hypothetical and conditional. Thus, for example, the natural sciences can teach us what we must do if we wish to master life technically, but they cannot and hence should not consider the question of whether or not it ultimately makes sense to do so. Jurisprudence can teach us which legal rule or procedure is best for attaining a given purpose, but it cannot and should not consider whether there should be such purposes and procedures. The historical and cultural sciences teach us to understand and interpret literary and social phenomena, but they dare not ask whether any given phenomenon is worthwhile. In sum, academicians may clarify values, but they dare not promulgate them within the walls of the academy. They may teach you that *if* you believe x you *must* believe y, and that *if* you want a given end you *must* also want certain inevitable means to it. But they may never engage ultimate questions of meaning without violating their vocational obligations.

Indeed, Weber insisted that questions of ultimate meaning and value *must not* be examined within the academy. If the kind of rationality proper to all of the academic disciplines is purely formal and never substantive, academics would seem to have no method and hence no warrant for weighing matters of ultimate concern. In addition, and more importantly, "Academic pleading [about ultimate questions] is meaningless in principle because the various value spheres of the world stand in irreconcilable conflict with one another."[14] Weber thus linked the notion of formal rationality to the doctrine of moral and religious relativism. Each one of these teachings warranted the other one, and both of them together conditioned the academic vocation. Weber thus forbade academics *qua academics* from examining ultimate questions, because there could be no academic justification for any answer that they might presume to give to such questions.

Weber's carefully circumscribed, even austere, account of the academic calling was but one instance of his more general account of the character of the *Berufsmensch,* the type of human being ideally suited to modern political, social, and economic conditions. Rogers Brubaker has argued persuasively that the constraints Weber placed upon academic inquiry were but a special case of the limits of the same formal rationality that governed the political and economic spheres of modern life. The virtues of friendship, brotherliness, and charity had, according to Weber, retreated from not only the economic and political spheres of life but from the academic sphere as well. Under such conditions, an impersonal, objective, and ascetic concept of vocation was, for Weber, the only adequate guide for action in a disenchanted world.[15]

Weber's rather abstract and forbidding account of the academic calling will probably not induce an immediate "shock of recognition" within most academics today. Practices and attitudes that are firmly embedded within academic institutions and forms of discourse do suggest, however, that Weber's image of the academic still holds most of us captive. I have already called attention to our collective sense that "our own work" really does refer only to research and publication. I would now call attention to several other revealing conventions and commonplaces of the academy.

Most of us are highly suspicious of colleagues who consider a concern with their students' overall well-being an integral part of their vocation. Some believe that it is simply imprudent to "waste so much time" over such matters. Others doubt whether academics are qualified to provide care and counsel of the sort that might be required really to nurture the souls of students. Few believe that academic advising should be rewarded; it seems to almost all faculty an irksome task at best. Friendship really has, for the most part, retreated from the realm of the classroom and the study (I will, perhaps mercifully, confine myself here to faculty/student relations; I will therefore not consider whether or not charity and friendship flourish within most academic departments).

And for whom do we write? Seldom for colleagues in our immediate midst, much less for our students, rarely for a general public. Most of us insist upon objective, distant, impersonal, and professional forms of review for "our work." Indeed, one of the reasons we often give for stressing publication is that we allegedly have mechanisms in place for "measuring the worth" of published work objectively and impersonally, whereas we believe we cannot appraise collegiality or teaching in such a "fair and thorough" manner.

Finally, many faculty members have been unable to find their own voices precisely because they experience alienation from "their own work" for exactly the reasons one might expect, given Weber's analysis of the academic calling. It does, after all, require a special kind of personality, not so much a special measure of intelligence, to write and at the same time will that your writing will be soon superseded. To view one's "work" as part of an *endless* process of rationalization, as a brick in an edifice of knowledge whose final shape one cannot in principle begin to imagine, is just to experience the Marxist sense of alienation from one's labor in a peculiarly acute form. In the meantime, the satisfactions that could and doubtless do give special meaning and purpose to the academic life—the face to face encounters that really do engage an enormous range of our human feelings and thoughts in a mutual and intimately collaborative search for insights and understandings that no participant possesses at the outset—are rare, evanescent, and, given the Weberian sense of vocation that we all more or less possess, vaguely suspect.

Perhaps more than any of his contemporary critics, Weber, in his bleakly knowing way, sensed much of this himself. In "Wissenschaft als Beruf" he claimed to be speaking "from precisely the standpoint that hates intellectualism as the worst devil." [16] But precisely because he had divested both the world (disenchantment) and the process of knowledge formation (*Wissenschaft* chained to the course of progress) of meaning, he had to invest the concept of *Beruf* with a meaning that the term had never possessed before him. The academic vocation became itself the source and the center of the meaning of academic life. Weber's academics surely did not work merely in order to live, nor did they live in order to work; rather, their work just *was* their life. And their salvation, the fate of their souls, depended upon their making correct conjectures, a making of knowledge that in turn depended partly upon a gift of grace or inspiration, and mainly upon the possession of firm and reliable methods.

In writing about salvation, gifts of grace, and the peculiar dignity inherent in Weber's ideal of the calling, I am not only following Weber, I am using a vocabulary whose principal terms were originally religious. More exactly, I am suggesting that Weber's sense of the academic vocation manifests a transvaluation of values, an appropriation and transmutation of religious language for distinctly secular purposes. I will therefore turn now to a consideration of the religious dimensions of the problem of the academic vocation today.

IV

At the same time that he was preparing "Wissenschaft als Beruf," Weber was revising what eventually became his most widely studied work, *The Protestant Ethic and the Spirit of Capitalism*. This coincidence, together with other revealing facts about Weber's personality and career, have led scholars to notice how much Weber's own conception of the academic vocation was based upon his earlier interpretation of Protestant worldly asceticism. Thus, for example, Arnold Eisen has argued that Weber's idea of Puritan asceticism shaped both the method and the substance of much of his sociological writings.[17] And Sheldon Wolin has demonstrated that Weber's Puritan actor was "the prototype for Weber's ideal types, Political Man and Scientific Man, and their respective vocations."[18]

My major aim here is to ponder the significance for us academics today of Weber's achievement in basing his conception of our task upon religious views of life even as he at the same time insisted that we must and do live in a world without God. Like much of Nietzsche's work, Weber's analysis of the academic vocation demonstrated the impossibly exacting, even absurd, psychological consequences of attempting to live out a Christian ethic absent any belief in the God of Christianity. But whereas Nietzsche proceeded from this demonstration to urge us to abandon the Christian *ethos* altogether, Weber urged us to retain the Protestant ethic while abandoning the system of religious beliefs that made such an ethic bearable. Indeed, Weber's account of our calling as academics can seem, for these reasons, alternatively ennobling and devastating.

Consider first of all Weber's pronouncement that all valuable academic work is highly specialized work. In *The Protestant Ethic,* Weber had shown that, for all Protestants, vocations were ordained by God for the purposes of ordering the world and serving humanity on earth. Division of labor was part of God's providence, and so Christians could find meaning in their vocations precisely because they could trust that God would orchestrate their separate and specialized endeavors into a kind of divine economy directed toward serving neighbors (Luther) or the common good (Puritan).[19] Thus, the Puritan *Berufsmensch* "neither inquires about nor finds it necessary to inquire about the meaning of his actual practice of a vocation within the whole world, the total framework of which is not his responsibility, but his God's."[20] In sum, the source of all callings was God and their collective end was human flourishing.

By contrast, the powers that bear down upon modern humans and that ordain their callings are not divine; rather, they are the inexorable conditions of modernity itself—specialization, rationalization, and intellectualization. Though the development of these conditions was linked historically (not logically or inevitably) to the Puritan ethic itself, their character is wholly secular. The specialized nature of the academic calling is then given, not by God, but by the "fate of our times."

To what human good or goods is specialized academic work directed?

Simply to the end of *Wissenschaft:* making knowledge. The specialized
products of academic work are not, however, part of a larger whole in
terms of which they can be said to have meaning and significance. Nor
can their value be understood in terms of some substantive goal beyond
themselves like human well-being or the public good. Whereas the
larger implication of their work had been left by the Puritans to God, "in
the modern setting, it is simply left. . . ."[21]

Sheldon Wolin has argued that the specialized academic became, for
Weber, a renunciatory hero.

> Like the Calvinist, scientific man accumulates, only his activity takes
> the form of knowledge; yet what he amasses has no more lasting value
> than other things of the world. Scientific knowledge is always being
> superseded. Finally, scientific man is also a renunciatory hero. His
> form of renunciation is dictated by the demands of specialization that
> require him to abandon the delights of the Renaissance and Goethian
> ideal of the universal man who seeks to develop many facets of his
> personality and as many different fields of knowledge as possible.[22]

Weber's academics had to renounce more than the ideal of universal
man, however. They had also to renounce, *in their callings,* spontaneous enjoyment, emotional satisfaction, and communal affections.
And again, academics had to subject themselves to this ascetic regimen
without the religious consolations, assurances, and commitments that
might have made sense of such self-abnegating behavior. "The Puritan," Weber wrote, "like every rational type of asceticism, tried to
enable a man to maintain and act upon his constant motives, especially
those which it taught him itself, against the emotions. . . . Contrary to
many popular ideas, the end of this asceticism was to be able to lead an
alert, intelligent life: the most urgent task the destruction of spontaneous, impulsive enjoyment, the most important means was to bring
order into the conduct of its adherents."[23] The constant motives of the
academic were, for Weber, supplied by the inner logic of the academic
disciplines themselves, and the true academic acted from a sense of duty
to these disciplines, never from purposes external to them, much less
from inclination or the pursuit of pleasure.

Like the Puritan *Berufsmensch,* modern academics gained a certain
measure of alertness, intelligence, even freedom, by virtue of devotion
to their callings, but they purchased them at enormous cost. By becoming more aware of the character of the forces that bore down upon them,

academics became less ignorant of their constraining hold. By practicing means-end rationality, they became clearer about the nature and the implications of their own values. And by systematic control over the spontaneous and emotional, they gained a certain measure of rational freedom, the ability to act from reasons rather than from impulse. Mastery of the world and self-mastery were interconnected.

The price of mastery, for the Weberian academic, was resigned acceptance, even advancement, of the retreat of "the ultimate and most sublime values" from academic life. Whereas Protestants had made the whole world and their own callings within it a sacred realm of God's providential care, academics systematically advanced the process of secularization. Weber himself was especially determined to control his own inclinations toward prophecy and moral exhortation within the academic sphere. As Don Levine has noted, Weber "experienced a deep conflict between the commitment to the professional norms of scientific work and an urge to play some kind of prophetic role."[24] He was perhaps less successful in managing this conflict in "Wissenschaft als Beruf" than in any of his other academic exercises. Thus, the address remains possibly the greatest prophecy against prophecy ever composed. On the other hand, he proclaimed to his dying day that "the intrusion of normative statements into scholarly questions is *the work of the Devil.*"[25]

Finally, the academic calling was, for Weber, a peculiarly anxious and lonely business. He had noted in *The Protestant Ethic* that the English Puritan's emphasis upon an "exclusive trust in God" had led him to issue "warnings against any trust in the aid of friendship of men."[26] And he had insisted that, in spite of the crucial importance of church membership for the Calvinist, "his intercourse with his God was carried on in deep spiritual isolation."[27] Indeed, Calvinism tended "to tear the individual away from the close ties with which he is bound to this world."[28] These accents carried over into Weber's own understanding of the modern academic calling as an impersonal and solitary undertaking. He invariably referred, when he spoke of the academic community, not to specific webs of human beings working in close personal relationship to one another, but to highly abstract entities such as fields of study, scientific disciplines, and forms of rationality.

Again, Weber's academic was even more acutely lonely than his Puritan precursor. However profound were the depths of the Puritan's spiritual isolation, he at least had intercourse with God. But the

Weberian academic could merely wait alone, in disciplined attention, for the chance infusion of mundane grace that would lead him to a temporary salvation through his making a correct conjecture in his manuscript. Peter Lassman and Irving Velody have summed these matters up very well. "In the disenchanted public world there can be no objective ranking of values, the scientist or the scholar can be no more certain of the value of science or scholarship than can the Calvinist be certain of election. The inner world of such a person is one threatened by anxiety and doubt in which those who 'live for' rather than 'live off' science are placed in an unbearable position."[29] And unlike the Calvinist, the Weberian academic had to bear this unbearable position alone.

Who among us present-day academics can live in such a manner? Few can, few do, few desire to do so. Most of us lack Weber's discipline and courage. But more to the point, Weber's academic is an ideal type, not a group profile. Furthermore, academics in the United States have grown accustomed to rhetorical strategies and institutional practices that have sought, from the beginnings of the modern research university in this country, to connect scholarly research to public service and the public good. I have examined Weber's ideal type at such length here in order to clarify many of the academic practices, internalized among us in habits of mind and language, that reward or otherwise tend to promote the kind of personality that Weber describes. To reinforce this point and to illustrate it further, let me now return briefly to the problems raised at the beginning of this chapter.

V

I began by noting three possible accounts of the meaning and purpose of the academic vocation—the cultivation of character (*Bildung* or formation), the transmission of knowledge and skills (information), and the making of knowledge (*Wissenschaft*). I suggested that faculty at Harvard and at other research universities currently understand "their own work" in terms of the third objective (*Wissenschaft*), and I observed that Harvard's recently retired president and other educators are now urging the modern university to think in terms of the first objective (formation), sometimes as distinct from or as opposed to the second (information). These matters, I said, were more complex than Bok suggests. It should now be easier to see why and how this is so.

In the first place, the transmission of knowledge is not obviously distinct from character formation, unless the former activity is construed as mere inculcation rather than as the development of a tradition of thought and learning. At the beginning of his 1983 Jefferson Lecture on the subject of tradition, Jaroslav Pelikan remarked upon an irony that he might have explained by referring to Weber. He noted that we are now "better equipped to deal with tradition than were our scholarly predecessors, although they and their audiences may have had a better concrete grasp of one or another of the specific traditions than we do." We have come to understand tradition at the very moment that "the home, the community, the school, and the church have all declined gravely in their ability (or willingness) to transmit one or another constituent element of the tradition."[30]

If my own analysis of Weber is at all correct, these ironies can to some extent be explained. Weber argued that *in order* to understand tradition we must rationalize it, must make it purely an object for impersonal inspection and formal analysis, and once we do that it ceases to be tradition for us. Pelikan has demonstrated that within the Christian tradition, for example, intellectuals have simultaneously thought about, criticized, and developed the tradition. Yet in spite of demonstrations like Pelikan's, the Weberians have temporarily prevailed; thus schools, especially universities, have declined in their willingness to transmit any kind of tradition. The activity has been reduced to the "transmission of knowledge and skills" (information or inculcation), and so it seems irrelevant to shaping the moral substance or the habits of mind and action that determine character.

I want to clarify this point further by offering a more concrete example. If I were to consider Weber's own complicated conception of rationality further than I have here, I should also consider thinkers like Luther, Calvin, Rousseau, Kant, Kierkegaard, and Dostoyevsky, all of whom had their own deep though differing senses of the powers and limits of reason. I would also need to engage contemporary feminist philosophers such as Elizabeth Minnich, who have offered thoroughgoing critiques of the narrowly circumscribed intellectual tradition that the aforementioned white males represent. In order really to study these thinkers, I must learn what they said, and I must consider whether what they said is true and important. To think about thinkers and texts *and* to think with them: this is conversation, the conversation of the present with its own past. To think *only* about a text *and* to claim that one cannot, as an academic, responsibly think with it: this is Weberianism. Weberian academics ask only whether what someone says about what a text means is true or false and what such a saying might imply. Tradition-minded academics ask these questions too, but they may also ask whether what a text says about how we are to live and what we are to do is true or false. Tradition-minded academics will not agree about the *answers* to these latter questions, but they can and should agree, against the Weberians, that such questions should be asked and answered truthfully throughout the academy. And in the course of this latter process, academics would most definitely help students "lead more ethical, fulfilling lives."

In the second place, I have tried to demonstrate that the academic vocation understood in terms of *Wissenschaft* finally does shape character or, more exactly, personality. Initially, making knowledge seems to preclude character formation, and it does indeed preclude or replace *Bildung*. But on Weber's account, the process of knowledge formation, if conducted rationally, really does favor and cultivate the emergence of a particular personality type. And this personality does exhibit virtues—clarity, but not charity; honesty, but not friendliness; devotion to the calling, but not loyalty to particular and local communities of learning. At the end of *The Protestant Ethic,* Weber seemed to warn us all against the appearance of personalities that would someday fully conform themselves to the ideal type of the worldly ascetic. "For of the last stage of this cultural development, it might well be truly said: 'Specialists without spirit, sensualists without heart; this nullity imagines that it has attained a level of civilization never before achieved.'"[31] The problem here is obvious: these are not the sorts of characters that Derek Bok wanted research universities to form.

Though the modern university has managed with remarkable success to institutionalize Weberianism since the time of "Wissenschaft als Beruf," contemporary thinkers, inside and outside the academy, have begun seriously to question the epistemological basis of Weber's account of the academic calling. Alasdair MacIntyre has insisted upon both the traditional character of all rationality and the rationality of all traditions. Parker Palmer has urged us to think of truth in terms of relationships. Richard Rorty has impelled the vocation of philosophy away from a quest for certainty and toward a process of edification. Wayne Booth has insisted that we should think of texts as potential friends and has given us the golden rule of hermeneutics: "Read as you would have others read you; listen as you would have others listen to you.'' Jeffrey Stout has sought to place "the critical study of religious ethics back on the intellectual agenda" of our times. This present-day discourse about higher learning among both the religious and the secular intellectuals in our midst should lead us not so much to solve the problems of the Weberian legacy as to reconceive them in fresh and productive ways.

I will accordingly consider in the next chapter these more recent cultural developments as various aspects and expressions of the resurgence of the question of community. I wish, however, to add one final word about the subject of the academic vocation before abandoning it as a topical focus. In a fine theological study of friendship and modern conceptions of vocation, Gilbert Meilaender has reminded us that "although some people seem to find their work satisfying in itself, it is equally true that 'work, for most people, has always been ugly, crippling, and dangerous.'''[32] The reminder is both bracing and salutary, as is the critique that follows:

> When the system of vocations as we experience it today is described in terms which make work the locus of self-fulfillment, Christian ethics ought to object—on the empirical ground that this is far from true, and on the theological ground that vocation ought not make self-fulfillment central. When work as we know it emerges as the dominant idea in our lives—when we identify ourselves to others in terms of what we do for a living, work for which we are paid—and when we glorify such work in terms of self-fulfillment, it is time for Christian ethics to speak a good word for working simply in order to live. Perhaps we need to suggest today that it is quite permissible, even appropriate, simply to work in order to live and to seek one's fulfillment elsewhere—in personal bonds like friendship, for example.[33]

Meilaender was not writing about the *Weberian* sense of the *academic* vocation with its peculiar sense of self-fulfillment through a kind of ascetic self-abnegation. Even so, his criticism pertains directly to the Weberian academic, even as it unintentionally suggests one of the more promising ways to reconceive the academic vocation today. What if the most enriching kinds of teaching and learning, reading and writing do entail friendship in a kind of extended Aristotelian sense? Then at least the academic vocation would be one in which the rigors of work and the pleasures of friendship could be united. I shall consider this and other possibilities in the two chapters that follow.

Notes

1. The most accessible source of the relevant portions of Bok's report is the brief excerpt published in the "Opinion" section of the *Chronicle of Higher Education* 34 (April 27, 1988), B4, and entitled " 'Universities Have an Obligation to Help Students Learn How to Lead Ethical, Fulfilling Lives.' "

2. Max Weber, "Science as a Vocation," in H. H. Gerth and C. Wright Mills, trans. and eds., *From Max Weber: Essays in Sociology* (Oxford University Press: New York, 1977), 129–56. Gerth and Mills have translated *Wissenschaft* as "science." Because *science* in the U.S. context is often understood to mean simply "natural science," and because the German word has a much wider range of reference, I have translated *Wissenschaft* as "academics." Weber was speaking about and referred to all of the academic disciplines in his 1918 address.

3. *Ibid.*, 135.

4. Ringer, *The Decline of the German Mandarins* (Harvard University Press: Cambridge, Mass., 1969), 87.

5. Jaspers quoted by Ringer, *op. cit.*, 106.

6. Jaspers again quoted by Ringer, *op. cit.*, 87.

7. Weber, "Science as a Vocation," 143.

8. Hugh Hawkins, "University Identity: The Teaching and Research Functions," in Alexandra Oleson and John Voss, eds., *The Organization of Knowledge in America: 1860–1920* (The Johns Hopkins University Press: Baltimore and London, 1979), 285–89. This important article provides an excellent account of the earliest efforts to distinguish, in both practical and theoretical terms, between teaching and original research. For two extensive studies of the German influence upon the development of research universities in the United States, see Laurence R. Vesey, *The Emergence of the American University* (University of Chicago Press: Chicago and London, 1974), esp. 121–79, and Richard Hofstadter and Walter P. Metzger, *The Development of Academic Freedom in the United States* (Random House: New York, 1955), 367–402. A more recent, sharply focused but nonetheless very instructive account of the German influence upon the University of Michigan challenges or modifies many of the important claims made by Vesey and Hofstadter; cf. James Turner and Paul Bernard, "The Prussian Road to the University? German Models and the University of Michigan, 1837–c. 1895," *Rackham Reports* (University of Michigan, 1988–89), 16.

9. *The Development of Academic Freedom*, 367.

10. Hugh Hawkins, *Between Harvard and America : The Educational Leadership of Charles W. Eliot* (Oxford University Press: New York, 1972), 3–33.

11. Weber, "Science as a Vocation," 155.

12. *Ibid.*, 139.

13. *Ibid.*, 137.

14. *Ibid.*, 147.

15. Brubaker, *The Limits of Rationality: An Essay on the Social and Moral Thought of Max Weber* (George Allen and Unwin: London, 1984), 28; 44.

16. Weber, "Science as a Vocation," 152.

17. Eisen, "Called to Order: The Role of the Puritan *Berufsmensch* in Weberian Sociology," *Canadian Journal of Sociology* 13 (1979), 203–18.

18. Wolin, "Max Weber: Legitimation, Method, and the Politics of Theory," *Political Theory* 9 (1981), 412.

19. Weber, *The Protestant Ethic and the Spirit of Capitalism,* trans. Talcott Parsons (Charles Scribner's Sons: New York, 1958), 160–61.

20. Weber, *Economy and Society: Essays in Sociology,* eds. and trans. Guenther Roth and Claus Wittich (Bedminster Press: New York, 1967), 548.

21. Eisen, "Called to Order," 214.

22. Wolin, "Max Weber," 413.

23. Weber, *The Protestant Ethic,* 119.

24. Levine, *The Flight from Ambiguity: Essays on Social and Cultural Theory* (University of Chicago Press: Chicago and London, 1987), 186.

25. Weber quoted by Levine, *op. cit.,* 192 (italics mine).

26. Weber, *The Protestant Ethic,* 106.

27. *Ibid.,* 106–7.

28. *Ibid.,* 108.

29. Lassman and Velody, "Max Weber on Science, Disenchantment and the Search for Meaning," in Lassmann and Velody, eds., *Max Weber's "Science as a Vocation"* (Urwin Hyman: London, 1989), 183.

30. Jaroslav Pelikan, *The Vindication of Tradition* (Yale University Press: New Haven and London, 1984), 5–6.

31. Weber, *The Protestant Ethic,* 182.

32. Meilaender, *Friendship: A Study in Theological Ethics* (University of Notre Dame Press: Notre Dame, 1981), 96.

33. *Ibid.,* 97.

2

Communities of Learning

I

Thus far I have tried to show that our present-day conception of the academic vocation is based at least in part upon the transmutation of ideas that were originally religious in origin and implication. In the next two chapters, I shall try to show why a reconception of the academic vocation should involve the reappropriation of certain religious virtues. I do not, however, intend this to be an atavistic undertaking: I have no patience for nostalgic returns to medieval syntheses of one sort or another. I shall accordingly argue in this chapter that what I take to be one of the main currents in contemporary thought—the resurgence of the question of community—both invites and to some extent warrants a religiously informed redescription of academic life and the academic vocation. In the next chapter, I will endeavor to provide just such a redescription as a corrective to the Weberian account I have already analyzed.

II

The resurgent interest in the question of community is an exceptionally broad phenomenon that embraces social and political theory, jurisprudence, theology, literary criticism, cultural anthropology, even the history and philosophy of science. I shall, however, restrict my attention here to the manner in which the community question impinges upon activities and aspirations that are central to the tasks of higher education—teaching, learning, knowledge, and truth. At the risk of drastic oversimplification, I will summarize this more restricted development as follows: over the course of the last twenty or so years, the question of community has replaced the epistemological question as foundational for all other inquiries. The answers to basic human questions, such as, What can we know? or How should we live? or In what or whom shall we place our hope? have come to depend, for a large number of intellectuals, upon the answer to a prior question, Who are *we?*

As a way of both documenting and deepening our sense of this decisive shift in the current climate of opinion, I propose to consider briefly two very influential books that appeared within four years of one another, Richard Rorty's *Philosophy and the Mirror of Nature* and Parker Palmer's *To Know As We Are Known.* Although the two books differ from one another in several important respects, they both concern themselves centrally with epistemological matters, and they converge from strikingly different directions upon the question of community. Rorty, a militant secular humanist, writes from a position at the very center of the academic establishment, yet his book, in spite of its sometimes very technical discourse, is still widely discussed outside the academy. Palmer, a committed Christian, writes from a position peripheral to the academic establishment, yet his book continues to find large and receptive audiences within the secular academy as well as outside it. Thus, the two books together both evince and advance the community question as the most vital theme within contemporary intellectual life.

Both Rorty and Palmer develop powerful arguments against the epistemological scheme that has dominated Western thought since at least the seventeenth century. Rorty, who refers to this scheme as the "mirror of nature" or "foundationalism," criticizes it from within the tradition of professional philosophy. Most of his book is a history of the unavailing efforts of philosophers, since the time of Descartes, to find certainty, to discover a set of sensations (raw feels or clear and distinct ideas) or terms (analytical truths, the symbols of mathematical logic) that would provide a secure foundation for all human inquiries and activities.

According to Rorty, philosophers have hoped to find a way of securing an absolute fit between our knowledge of the world and the world itself, to show that in at least *one* area of intellectual endeavor human knowledge really does "mirror" reality. And for most of the last 350 years this effort to ground all human knowledge has focused upon the physical sciences; indeed, "since the period of Descartes and Hobbes, the assumption that scientific discourse was normal discourse and that all other discourse needed to be modeled upon it has been the standard motive for philosophizing." [1]

Rorty not only demonstrates that the foundationalist project has, in its own terms, failed; he also shows how it led philosophy to abandon its proper subject. Through arguments that are too intricate and extensive to summarize here, Rorty shows how a series of philosophers, especially Dewey, Wittgenstein, and Heidegger, but also including Wilfred Sellars, Hilary Putnam, and Thomas Kuhn, have exposed foundationalism as a fundamentally misguided effort. But Rorty is even more interested in the baleful effects of foundationalism than he is in charting its collapse. "The Cartesian change from mind-as-reason to mind-as-inner-area," he writes,

> was not the triumph of the prideful individual subject freed from scholastic shackles so much as the triumph of the quest for certainty over the quest for wisdom. From that time forward, the way was open for philosophers either to attain the rigor of the mathematician or the mathematical physicist, or to explain the appearance of rigor in these fields, rather than to help people attain peace of mind. Science, rather than living, became philosophy's subject, and epistemology its center. [2]

Palmer, to some extent like Rorty, begins with a critique of the dominant epistemological scheme of the last three centuries. Palmer calls this scheme "objectivism," and he describes it not so much in terms of a history of ideas or a group of thinkers as in terms of a set of pedagogical practices that characterizes the contemporary academy. [3] Thus, Palmer's focus remains in one respect broader and in another respect narrower than Rorty's. Its comparative breadth consists in Palmer's attention to the way in which most teachers teach, regardless of whether they are teaching philosophy, literature, religion, or physics. Palmer's critique extends to practices far beyond the narrower confines of professional philosophy. On the other hand, Palmer's "objectivism" refers to the dominant strain or to an amalgam of two strains (empiricism and a certain kind of pragmatism) within the larger epistemological project that Rorty calls the "mirror of nature." These distinctions are important, because they help in part to explain why Rorty finally argues for an abandonment of epistemology altogether, whereas Palmer seeks to replace or superscde objectivism with another epistemology.

The sources of Palmer's critique of modern epistemology are very different from Rorty's. Whereas Rorty relies exclusively upon philosophical writings that have subverted the foundationalist project, Palmer draws primarily upon Christian classics and upon a tradition of Christian spirituality that he traces back to the desert fathers. Moreover, Palmer's indictment of objectivism stems from his insight that epistemologies have moral trajectories, that ways of knowing are not morally neutral but morally directive. Objectivism, he demonstrates, places the would-be knower in an alienated, even an antagonistic position over and against the known world. Impelled by curiosity and the mania for control, objectivism fractures the bonds of community and tends inherently toward violence.[4] In view of this violent trajectory of objectivism, "we must," Palmer argues, "recover from our spiritual tradition the models and methods of knowing as an act of love."[5]

Yet another apparent difference between Rorty and Palmer reveals, upon closer scrutiny, the presence of a common spirit or at least a common undertaking between the two men, one that manifests itself most fully in something of a quest for community. Palmer always uses the term *objective* to describe an antagonistic posture between the isolated, active knower who seeks, for purposes of manipulation and control, to grasp, through the scientific method, the passive objects of the world in such a way that the knowledge that results "will reflect the nature of the objects in question rather than the knower's whims."[6] Rorty, on the other hand, observes that we use the term *objective* sometimes to mean "representing things as they really are" and at other times to designate "the presence of, or the hope for, agreement among inquirers."[7] He argues that these two meanings are by no means coextensive, and he decidedly prefers the latter to the former designation. Indeed, according to Rorty's own preferred view of knowledge, "epistemological behaviorism" as he somewhat unfelicitously calls it, "we understand knowledge when we understand the social justification of belief, and thus have no need to view it as accuracy of representation."[8]

Though this view is by no means identical to the one that Palmer advocates, some affinities between the two are quite striking. For example, Palmer insists that both *knowledge* and *truth* are communal terms. Knowledge is not the result of the isolated individual's efforts to mirror the world; it is instead a form of responsible relationship, even a "means to relationship," with others.[9] Knowing "becomes a reunion of separated beings whose primary bond is not of logic but of love"; truth is the name of this "community of relatedness."[10] For Rorty, once we see knowledge as a matter of conversation and of social practice, rather than as an attempt to mirror nature, truth is "what is *good for us* to believe" rather than privileged "contact with reality."[11] However much they may differ on other matters, both Rorty and Palmer understand knowledge and community as correlative terms.

They both also absorb aspects of the projects that they criticize into the fabric of the enterprises that they promote. Thus, Palmer recognizes that the objectivist project has "helped to untangle some very twisted strands of the human soul."[12] And he retains in his own epistemological scheme objectivism's honorable opposition to self-centeredness. Rorty wishes to retain epistemological behaviorism's understanding of objectivity, even as he argues for the abandonment of epistemology-centered philosophy in favor of hermeneutics.

Rorty's description of the hermeneutical or edifying philosopher resembles Palmer's description of the knower-in-community. Instead of passing judgment upon which discourses are rational and which are not, or seeking to "ground" all discourse in a common set of terms or procedures, the hermeneutical philosopher "sees the relations between various discourses as those of strands in a possible conversation, a conversation which presupposes no disciplinary matrix which unites the speakers, but where the hope of agreement is never lost so long as the conversation lasts. This hope is not a hope for the discovery of antecedently existing common ground, but simply hope for agreement, or, at least, exciting and fruitful disagreement."[13] Above all else, the edifying philosopher takes responsibility for keeping this conversation alive, not by "finding the proper set of terms into which all the contributions should be translated," but by being willing "to pick up the jargon of the interlocutor, rather than translating it into one's own."[14] The participants in this conversational endeavor—this *societas*—are "persons whose paths through life have fallen together, united by civility rather than by a common goal, much less a common ground."[15]

Rorty and Palmer do not finally share a "common ground" (a matter that I shall reconsider at a later point). I have nevertheless tried to discern here, by tacking back and forth between them and noting certain revealing points of intersection, the shape of the conversation that pro-

vides the current context for discussion about religion and higher education. The most important feature of that context seems to be the very
recent but very striking ascendancy of the community question over all
others. Before attempting to advance the discussion about religion and
higher education within this context, and because the context itself
seems so novel, I think it is important to enlarge the historical perspective upon our present situation by way of providing some correctives to
the historical accounts that are either supplied or implied by Rorty and
Palmer. Developing these correctives will also sharpen the features of
some of the problems that are peculiar to our present situation.

III

Let me begin by stating as succinctly as I can the story of how we came
to this present pass. The outlines of what Rorty calls foundationalism
and what Palmer calls objectivism were developed during the seventeenth century by thinkers such as Descartes, Hobbes, and Locke. But
two centuries elapsed before these ideas attained cultural dominion in
the West (or in at least the Anglo-American portion of it). That dominion was completed by four concurrent and overlapping developments:
the rise of professionalism, the emergence of the academic disciplines as
we know them today, the making of the modern research university, and
the shift from a mechanistic (because based upon physics) to a developmental (because based upon Darwinian biology) view of knowledge and
culture.

During this same period (roughly 1870–1900), however, there arose
several powerful critiques of the dominant, because recently institutionalized, epistemology. Nietzsche inaugurated one line of criticism
that has continued through the works of Heidegger and Gadamer.
William James began another one that has continued through Dewey and
the Chicago pragmatists to Quine and Rorty. These various lines have by
now collectively mounted a formidable challenge to foundationalism,
but the institutional superstructures that secured foundationalism's triumph remain intact. We stand in something of the same position relative
to antifoundationalism as was once occupied by early nineteenth-century
American colleges relative to foundationalism. We are, to speak in
sociological terms, in a period of cultural lag, or, as the poet Matthew
Arnold put it, we are "caught between two worlds, the one dead, the
other powerless to be born."

It is important to stress that the two dominant lines of criticism noted here began during the 1870s and 1880s at precisely the same time that the modern research university emerged as a new institution of higher learning in America. Palmer, though he recognizes the appearance of significant dissent from the objectivist position, suggests that it has been only recently developed and voiced.[16] And partly for this reason, he amalgamates one of these dissenting lines, pragmatism, with empiricism to describe objectivism.

Pragmatism, however, at least the pragmatism of William James, actually arose as a sharp protest against the kind of thinking that Palmer calls objectivism but which was called *positivism* at the time that James was writing in the 1870s and 1880s. Thus, for example, James's earliest writings contain detailed attacks against what he called the "correspondence theory of truth."[17] He always insisted that we are "coefficients" of the truth we seek to know, neither alienated from nor antagonistic to the world of which we are a part. He moreover argued that the "whole man is at work within us"—our feelings, our faiths, our intuitions, and our hopes, as well as our thoughts and theories—when we seek knowledge.[18] He was, as all of his writings attest, an unrelenting enemy of the objectivist or positivist account of knowing as a mere matter of logic and dispassionate reasoning.[19]

Palmer ignores this Jamesean strain of pragmatism, because his own thinking was shaped, as he tells us in one of the most powerfully confessional portions of his book, by a different strand of the pragmatic tradition. He came to believe that knowledge emerges through the imposition of order upon the chaos of experience, and that truth is just a name for whatever "works" to solve certain problems, for whatever eventuates in a satisfactory manipulation of the world.[20] This vulgarly practical and relativistic theory of truth perhaps most closely approximates the current, popular sense of the word *pragmatic,* and one can find warrants for it in the writings of all the pragmatists, even including some of James's.

Nevertheless, as Richard Bernstein has observed, the American pragmatists—especially Peirce, James, and Dewey—had already formulated an antifoundational approach to philosophy before the First World War. In addition, they had emphasized the "social character of the self and the need to nurture a critical community of inquirers."[21] What Peirce long ago wrote about philosophers applies today to all of those who seek to discover knowledge and truth. Because, according to Peirce, our understanding of matters is invariably fallible and partial—

both in the sense of "biased" and in the sense of a seeing only a part—
"we individually cannot reasonably hope to attain the ultimate philosophy which we pursue; we can only seek it, therefore, for the *community*
of philosophers."[22]

In sum, we should not permit the cultural ascendancy, during most of
the twentieth century, of a vulgar strain of pragmatism to obscure the
very promising alternatives to objectivism that were developed by
Peirce, James, and others as early as 1880. One strain of pragmatism has
combined with empiricism to produce objectivism. But another strain of
pragmatism—its most original strain, and one that is still discernible in
Rorty—is very congenial to Palmer's own critique of objectivism.

There is, however, another and better reason why Palmer ignored
James and other late-nineteenth-century critics of objectivism: he did not
set out to write a piece of intellectual history. Rather, as noted earlier, he
derived objectivism from current pedagogical practice, and he never
intended to suggest that objectivism, in the complete sense of the word,
could be found in the writings of any given thinker or set of thinkers. Yet
if Palmer is correct, as I think he is, in taking objectivism to be *the*
epistemology that informs the practices of the modern university, and if
I am correct in suggesting that James and others had already fashioned
powerful alternative theories of knowledge as early as 1880, a vital
historical question arises. How, given the presence of several conflicting
epistemologies, did one of them come to dominate the modern university?

We might expect to receive an answer to this question from Rorty,
who is explicitly and deliberately historical in a way that Palmer is not.
Rorty's history is, however, purely "internalist" by design. He attends
only to the development of ideas within the discipline of philosophy, not
to external considerations—social, economic, technological, and political—that impinged in various ways upon that development and doubtless propelled it in certain directions. Though a complete historical
explanation of the ascendancy of objectivism or foundationalism would
require an analysis of all of these conditions, only one of them, the
political factor, is crucially relevant to my present purpose.

That purpose is to issue an emphatic historical reminder to all of us
who criticize the ethos of objectivism in the name of communitarian
accounts of knowledge and truth. The principal dangers inherent in
communitarianism are tribalism and the subsequent violence that often
arises among rival tribes, each of them inflexibly wedded to their respec-

tive versions of the truth. I would argue that objectivism arose initially
and that it subsequently attained cultural dominion primarily because it
was intended by its architects as a way of *avoiding* violence. We must at
least add the desire for civil peace to the two desires, curiosity and
control, that Palmer has identified as the motives for objectivism.

Hobbes and Descartes manifested this pacific motive most vividly of
all the seventeenth-century advocates of objectivism or foundationalism. "Fear and I were born twins," Hobbes said, remarking upon the
fact that his birthday fell on the same day that England trembled under
the onslaught of the Spanish Armada. When he developed the objectivist
epistemology that encompassed the first part of *Leviathan,* when he
argued, contrary to all of the ancients, that nature "dissociates," he did
so, against the background of civil war, primarily to secure a rational
foundation for politics so that such wars could be avoided in the future.[23]

While Hobbes was brooding over the growing civil strife in England,
Descartes was in winter quarters with the French army in Germany,
where the "fortune of war" had taken him. There he retreated alone into
a stove-heated room "to look for the true method of attaining knowledge
of everything [his] mind could grasp."[24] Again, as we can see from the
autobiographical account Descartes gives us in his seminal *Discourse on
the Method of Rightly Directing One's Reason and of Seeking Truth in
the Sciences,* the quest for certain and secure foundations began, as it
had with Hobbes, in part as a stay against the confusion and violence
borne of religious conflict.

Philosophers such as Stephen Toulmin and Jeffrey Stout have recently
emphasized the importance of religious conflict as the background to
foundationalist enterprises. Indeed, Stout has made the religious wars of
the seventeenth century the pivotal episode in his subtle and searching
narrative of the rise of modern moral thought. While I welcome these
historical reminders as supplements to Rorty and correctives to Palmer, I
wish to note here that the unprecedented violence of the twentieth century does not, for some reason, figure prominently in Stout's account of
the gradual undermining of foundationalism. Thus, whereas Palmer may
need to be reminded of the violence borne of *religious conflict,* Stout
needs to be reminded of the violence borne of *secular* ideologies. It
seems unbalanced at best to ascribe the rise of foundationalist projects in
part to the inability of religious groups to manage conflict without resort-
ing to violence and then to ignore altogether, in the course of an account

of the collapse of foundationalism, the failure of modern nation states, informed by traditions that are self-consciously secular, to resolve conflicts short of world war. To update and correct Whitehead here, the religious wars of the seventeenth century seem like tempests in a teapot compared to the wars and revolutions of the twentieth. Toulmin, unlike Stout, gives equal emphasis to economic, social, and religious conflict as a background to the change in "philosophy's agenda" after about 1630. But he too understands the new agenda as a quest for coherence and peace in the face of violent strife and confusion.[25]

Objectivism as the best *alternative* to violence: both Rorty and Palmer ignore this important truth about the epistemological tradition they criticize, though they do so for different reasons. Rorty ignores it, because he is concerned only with the internal history of modern philosophy. Palmer ignores it, because he believes that in order to account for the violent trajectory of objectivism, he must find exclusively egoistic motivation—idle curiosity and the desire for control—as the basic impetus behind it.

I do not mean to suggest here that Rorty and Palmer ignore the virtues of the Enlightenment altogether, much less that either is antagonistic to them. Indeed, as noted earlier, they both incorporate some elements of objectivism into their own prescriptions. Palmer, moreover, openly insists that we must not romanticize the life of "the earlier [premodern] world [which] was often little more than a reflection of the passions and prejudices of those who claimed to know."[26] And Rorty states flatly that "the preservation of the values of the Enlightenment is our best hope."[27]

But by ignoring or at least underestimating the extent to which objectivism's vices are precisely the defects of its virtues, both Rorty and Palmer are more sanguine than the historical record warrants in believing that one can persuasively disentangle the sinister strands of objectivism from its more humane strands within the academic conscience of the West. Any radical alternative to foundationalism or objectivism will seem to open up the prospect of renewed violence among different communities who would seem to have no *rational foundation* on the basis of which they might adjudicate the disagreements that might arise among them.

There may very well be a way successfully to assuage this fear of violence, and I think that Palmer at least has partially succeeded in doing so. But those who welcome the supersession of the epistemological

question by the community question need to recognize how deep seated
and how historically well founded are the fears of foundationalists who
believe that if objectivism disappears, force, not some new epistemology, will take its place. This fear of tribalism and violence is perhaps the
foremost difficulty that most communitarian accounts of knowledge
must face.

IV

Though I myself welcome the recent cultural ascendancy of the community question, I need to admit and then to face honestly two further
difficulties that have attended this development before I can then proceed, in the next chapter, to demonstrate the need for the cultivation of
certain religious virtues within communities of higher learning. These
two difficulties should already be apparent from my brief account of
Palmer and Rorty. First, the concept of community needs further specifi-
cation. Second, the relationship between community on the one hand
and knowledge and truth on the other hand needs further elucidation. In
the course of addressing these difficulties, I will anchor my discussion
firmly within the actual experiences of common life within the present-
day academy.

Much of the discussion of community today is marked by a degree of
imprecision that borders on obscurity. Most parties to the discussion
exhibit a terminological wavering of the sort that once characterized the
discussion of culture among anthropologists. In the latter conversation,
some thought of Culture (invariably with a capital *C*) as a unitary concept of an ideal and then proceeded to determine how much Culture any
given group possessed. Others insisted that the topic could only be
fruitfully pursued if one spoke of cultures, always in the lowercase
plural and always designating empirical realities, to refer to all groups
who shared a common language and a common past or identity.[28] Still
others oscillated between the grand ideal of Culture (variously described) and the actual diversity of groups, all of them cultures but
possessing no discernible "essence" in common.

Conversation about community over the course of the last century has
paralleled the conversation about culture. Thus, Dewey, one of the
philosophers who have most influenced Rorty, sometimes spoke of publics or communities in the plural to refer to any group of people that

recognizes itself as having some common problem or another. Under this description communities are kaleidoscopic, evanescent entities, assuming temporary shape and then dissolving once the problems that gave them their original purpose have disappeared or been resolved. On the other hand, Dewey spoke of the search for the "Great Community" or "Public," and these were terms that designated his special sense of democracy itself.[29]

Rorty's own notions of community are much more obscure than Dewey's. He never actually uses *community* as a significant analytical category, but he constantly refers to collectivities of one sort or another in his effort to substantiate what he takes to be the only defensible understanding of knowledge (what is warrantably assertible by us) and truth (whatever is good for us to believe). Thus, he speaks of the subjective conditions of inquiry of any kind as "just the facts about what a given society, or profession, or other group, takes to be good ground for assertions of a certain sort." Rorty then refers to all of these collectivities as "disciplinary matrices."[30] This bewildering parade of names indicates that the dialectics of Dewey (his movement back and forth between the ideal and the reality of community) has degenerated, in Rorty's hands at least, into sheer obscurantism.

Let me begin to demystify matters here by articulating some obvious truths. Academies are places of learning. Students and faculty come together, because they seek knowledge and understanding. It may well be that many, perhaps most, students go to colleges and universities for other purposes; nevertheless, the two constitutive functions of academies are teaching and learning. These functions in turn include a variety of activities—reading, writing, computing, memorizing—that purport to advance disciplined thinking about important matters of human concern.

All disciplined thinking, even when it proceeds, as most of it does, in the solitary confines of the study, derives from and therefore depends upon social processes such as language and tradition. Moreover, disciplined thought is itself often dialogical (involving two inner voices), more often conversational (involving many such voices). The eminent British philosopher of education R. S. Peters has stated this latter and by now commonplace point as elegantly as anyone:

> Plato once described philosophy as the soul's dialogue with itself. It is
> a pity that this clue was not followed up. For the notion would not then
> have developed that reason is a sort of mental gadget that can be

> used by the individual or, as Hume described it, a "wonderful and
> unintelligible instinct in our souls." The ability to reason, in the
> philosophical sense of thinking critically about one's beliefs, develops
> only if a man keeps critical company so that a critic is incorporated in
> his own consciousness. The dialogue within is inseparable from the
> dialogue without.[31]

This image of the individual disciplined thinker as engaged in a process that is in a derivative sense communal outlines some of the central
and ideal features of *academic* community. First, this community is
intentional in that it aims at knowledge and truth. Second, just as the
voices within converse with one another in an intimate, critical, and
engaging manner, so too must students and faculty treat one another
with critical respect and concern. Like disciplined thought itself, community flourishes or perishes depending not only upon the critical acu-
men of the various voices of which it is composed but also upon the
extent to which and the manner in which they respect and listen to one
another.

Of all the gatherings on a university campus, classroom meetings
would seem most closely to approximate the ideal features of academic
community just outlined. Like Dewey's emerging publics, these meetings arise around a set of questions or problems or subject matters. And
they are surely evanescent. But unlike Dewey's publics, classroom
meetings end, not when a given problem has disappeared or been resolved but when a bell rings or a term concludes. Like the internal
conversation that is disciplined thought, classroom meetings do aim at
knowledge, truth, and understanding. But many, perhaps most, classroom meetings do not include much conversation, nor is there, for the
most part, much intimacy and engagement among the several members
of the group.

It therefore seems strained at best to speak of most classrooms as
communities; perhaps they are best described, to borrow a term from
cultural anthropology, as focused gatherings. Yet they are nevertheless
the single, most important element in the overall assemblage of groups
that constitutes the academic community, for the classroom is the place
where students learn the disciplines and the virtues that are necessary to
participate in a community of learning. In short, every teacher is teaching at least two things in every classroom: his or her subject and the
manners of learning. I use the term *manners* here deliberately to capture
both the sense of *methods* and the sense of *virtues*.

Flourishing beyond the classrooms are a bewildering number of academic assemblies—faculty groups, sometimes defined along departmental lines, sometimes not; informal gatherings of students in residence halls and other locations; and any number of groups, comprising both students and faculty, who congregate for the purpose of learning together. Faculty members are the most crucial element in this assemblage of groups, because they, more than the students, give shape and substance to the entire configuration of groups, because they are relatively more permanently rooted within any given academy, and because they are charged with the task of initiating the students into the discourses and the disciplines, the subjects and the manners, of higher learning.

In brief, any academic community is itself an assemblage of groups that can be designated "communities," not because they possess a common essence but because they display a certain family resemblance to one another. Even so, there are some basic outlines that circumscribe academic communities: their face-to-face quality, their common pursuit of knowledge and understanding, and their integral character, the sense in which the quality of the individual's thought and the quality of the communities' thinking are mutually dependent upon one another. The excellence of "the dialogue within is inseparable from [the excellence of] the dialogue without."

When Parker Palmer claims that knowing is a "reunion of separated beings whose primary bond is not of logic but of love" or that knowledge is itself a form of responsible relationship, he intends, I think, to call attention to this integral character of the community of learning. When Rorty argues that "we understand knowledge when we understand the social justification of belief," he too means to emphasize the irreducibly communal dimension of thought. Even so, both Palmer and Rorty occasionally mystify and perplex readers who need greater clarity about the exact connections between community on the one hand and knowledge and truth on the other. I will therefore turn now to this second difficulty that has arisen recently in the context of the community question.

Academic community does not refer to some sort of metaphysical entity that is prior to the individuals of which it is made up and free from its own history and traditions. It is instead, as I have been suggesting, a configuration of plural communities with their own conventions, disciplinary histories, standards of evidence and argument, and patterns of

discourse. So we need not conjure up, in thinking through the relationships among community, knowledge, and truth, assortments of alche-
mists or flat-earthers as plausible examples of communities of inquirers
within the contemporary academy. Inquiry takes place within academic
communities that are themselves embedded within an epistemic context,
which context conditions in large part the justification of belief. To
know something is just to hold beliefs about it that are justified. Justification of belief is itself a communal endeavor, the outcome, if you
will, of disciplined inquiry.

Though communal inquiry secures knowledge through internal processes of justification, it does not ensure truth. Inquiries can go wrong in
many ways and for many reasons. Even so, as Jeffrey Stout has well
said,

> Truth is a property of interpreted sentences, and interpreted sentences
> belong to languages which are human creations. The world-as-it-is-in-
> itself is, by definition, the world apart from the application of inter-
> preted sentences by human beings—the world described for epis-
> temological purposes as undescribed. It therefore includes no truths.
> To accept or discover the truth about something is to have acquired a
> language in which interpreted sentences can be applied in a certain
> way. It is therefore to make use of human artifice, to possess certain
> habits, beliefs, and so on. That is the only road to truth about
> anything.[32]

Academic communities are interpretive and self-critical. But though
they aim at knowledge and truth, their capacity really to discover the
truth about any matter will depend, as Stout here suggests, in part upon
their possession of certain vocabularies, skills, and virtues. In other
words, precision about truth and knowledge is itself contingent upon the
understanding of the particular contexts within which these terms are
used. For this reason, Parker Palmer is correct when he argues that
community and *truth* are correlative terms.

Because he, like Stout, recognizes that the discovery of truth depends
upon the possession of certain virtues and skills, Parker Palmer is, by
comparison to Rorty, quite lucid on the subject of community. I noted
earlier that Palmer and Rorty do not finally share a "common ground,"
primarily because Palmer is rooted in a spiritual tradition and Rorty is
not. For this reason, and because of Palmer's long experience of living
in community, he can speak on the subject with far greater clarity and
authority than Rorty. Indeed, I would argue that in general the religious

are best situated to advance Western culture's understanding of community. And this is no small opportunity, given the fact that the secular part of Western culture has itself raised the community question with such unprecedented urgency.

But what besides Palmer's tradition and experience accounts for his clear conception of community? It seems initially as though Palmer's discussion of community inscribes a wider arc than even Dewey's, to embrace on the one hand the interrelatedness and wholeness of all of the original creation and on the other hand the difficult and sharply focused achievement of living in intimate association with a particular group of human beings. But instead of dissipating into Rortyesque vagueness, Palmer's analysis becomes very concrete and very instructive through his understanding of community as the place where some very specific spiritual virtues are nurtured and practiced. The practice of these virtues in turn makes possible the conception of knowledge that Palmer defends.

Palmer's understanding of community thus begins precisely where Rorty's ends, with a group of people, a *societas* in Rorty's terms, whose "paths through life have fallen together." More exactly, these persons have gathered together in a classroom for the purpose of learning, and it is up to the teacher, in Palmer's judgment, "to create a space in which obedience to truth is practiced."[33] This creation of community involves the cultivation of certain virtues through certain disciplines and pedagogical practices. I must admit that Palmer sometimes invests the classroom with certain mystical possibilities that I find puzzling. Though like Palmer I think of classroom activity as a training ground for disciplined thought, I have a somewhat less exalted sense of its possibilities; I doubt seriously that any one classroom can be considered a fully realized community. For me the strength and therefore the authority of Palmer's analysis of community derives primarily from his understanding of character, from what in his terms might best be called spiritually grounded habits of mind.

I have tried to show here that in our present circumstances the clarification of the concept of academic community and the elucidation of knowledge and truth are closely related enterprises. To ask about the meaning of truth is to raise questions about context, about the boundaries, the vocabulary, and the virtues that collectively define the shape and the substance of a particular community of inquirers whose primary intention is to discover the truth. Once the epistemological center of gravity has shifted to a place outside the self, questions about communal ideals and questions about knowledge and truth are, though not identical, ineluctably convergent.

V

Before I turn to an extensive discussion of the relationship between religious virtues and higher learning, I must address a fourth and final difficulty that attends the contemporary conversation about community. Michael Ignatieff has framed this critique as forcefully as anyone:

> Words like fraternity, belonging and community are so soaked with nostalgia and utopianism that they are nearly useless as guides to the real possibilities of solidarity in modern society. Modern life has changed the possibilities of civic solidarity, and our language stumbles behind like an overburdened porter with a mountain of old cases. . . . Our task is to find a language for our need for belonging which is not just a way of expressing nostalgia, fear and estrangement from modernity.[34]

Jeffrey Stout has discerned some of these same nostalgic impulses at work among the communitarians and has suggested that many of them suffer from "terminal wistfulness."[35] And Jeremy Waldron, who was himself persuaded by Ignatieff's critique among others, has noted repeatedly that terms like *brotherhood* and *community* are now merely codewords that timid or estranged souls use to protest modernity.[36]

All three of these critics are speaking about civic life, but their misgivings about community apply as well to my discussion of academic life in communitarian terms. Ignatieff continues his critique of communitarians with a question: "Our political images of civic belonging remain haunted by the classical polis, by Athens, Rome, and Florence. Is there a language of belonging adequate to Los Angeles?" I might well ask, given my present purposes, "Is there a language of community adequate to UCLA?"[37]

No and yes. No, because UCLA, along with any number of other large research-oriented universities, embodies, in its practices and its language, the Weberian ethos I described in the previous chapter. And, as I have shown, Weber himself shaped the self-understanding of the modern academy by creating much of its vocabulary. He did so, moreover, by insisting that the academic realm, like the political and economic realms, had become and would remain governed by means-end rationality and by impersonal constraints. Like Ignatieff, Weber believed that talk of friendship, community, and a sense of belonging was best consigned to private life. Up to a point, Weber and Ignatieff would surely be right: UCLA *as a whole* cannot be adequately analyzed by the language of community.

But matters are more complicated than this. One of UCLA's own faculty members has written a historical study of civic life in early modern Philadelphia that is germane to my own analysis of his and others' academic lives at UCLA. Gary B. Nash has noted that in pre-Revolutionary days, Philadelphia was in some sense a single community. But over time its population increased, its class divisions became more pronounced, its ethnic composition became more diverse, its neighborhoods changed their configurations, and its economic system became more geared to the impersonality of the marketplace. Unlike some historians who, in view of these developments, proclaim the loss of community in Philadelphia, Nash argues for another analytical strategy. "Rather than nostalgically tracing the eclipse of community," he writes, "we need to trace the continuously evolving process of community." Nash then proceeds to discuss craft organizations, working-class taverns, benevolent societies, free black churches, and reform associations. Instead of dismissing these structured organizations as mere *Gesellschaften,* Nash assigns to them a leading role in the creation of genuine urban community, of what he calls *"Gemeinschaft* of mind— the mental life of community."[38]

Although analogies drawn between civic and academic life are far from perfect, I would insist that something like Nash's analysis of Philadelphia better captures the fabric of his and others' academic lives at UCLA than does the language of *Gesellschaft.* UCLA is simply less than the sum of its parts. Its intellectual vitality arises not at the level of the university as a whole but from the myriad communities whose assemblage we designate UCLA. And these communities are marked by features I have outlined as circumscribing the family of communities that constitutes any college or university: face-to-face engagement, aspirations to knowledge and truth, and integral relationships between individual thought and communal conversation.

Neither the language of *Gesellschaft* nor the language of *Gemeinschaft* can adequately describe the modern academy. The two vocabu-

laries arose initially, in the writings of Ferdinand Tonnies, in a kind of
dialectical opposition to one another. Indeed, it would be a subtle historical task to determine whether the language of community arose as a
protest against modernity or whether the language of modernity arose as
a protest against what were taken to be the utopian impulses behind the
language of community.[39] At any rate, Tonnies, who first coined the
word *Gemeinschaft* as a sociological category, used the term in both
a descriptive and a critical sense. "His images of *Gemeinschaft*,"
Harry Liebersohn has shown, "were not an inducement to nostalgia so
much as a powerful reminder of things that once had been and could
return."[40]

To criticize communitarian thought *simply* because it deploys images
drawn from a real or imagined past as criticism of the present is to
dismiss arbitrarily much of modern social and political theory. Are we to
disregard Rousseau's *Discourse on the Origins of Inequality* because of
his invocation of a state of nature and a subsequent state of nascent civil
society? Are we to dismiss Thomas Paine because he takes us back to
Eden on the road to establishing the rights of man? If thinkers as diverse
as Rousseau, Paine, and Tonnies are all to be understood as utopian
insofar as they criticize the present from the standpoint of a real or
imagined past, then utopianism is an honored mode of cultural criticism.

So too is *bricolage*, the borrowing from various vocabularies, some
contemporary, others retrieved from the past and revivified, in order to
fashion a critical redescription of a form of human life. This will be my
project in the next chapter. In the course of my redescription of academic life, I shall not suggest that we should refashion UCLA into a
Platonic academy. That *would* be nostalgic utopianism. But I will be
borrowing images and ideals from religious thinkers and from religious
communities of learning. As I have tried to show, contemporary discourse about community, much of it wholly secular in character, both
invites and warrants this undertaking.

The task is invited, because communitarian accounts of knowledge
and truth have undermined the epistemology that informed Weber's
conception of the academic calling. And that conception involved, as I
have shown, a transmutation, sometimes a subversion, of terms that
were religious in origin and implication. The task is warranted, because
communitarians are often insufficiently attentive to the affections and
the virtues that are required in order to keep disciplined communal
conversation flourishing. Rorty's analysis of community is weak in part

because he lacks a spiritual tradition within which he can ground it, and Palmer's spiritually grounded analysis is strongest where it is informed by his discussion of certain specific virtues and disciplines. I believe, therefore, that the most promising argument for an integral relationship between religion and higher education can be made through a demonstration that the practice of certain spiritual virtues is and has always been essential to the process of learning, even within the secular academy.

Notes

1. Richard Rorty, *Philosophy and the Mirror of Nature* (Princeton University Press: Princeton, 1979), 387.

2. *Ibid.*, 61.

3. Parker Palmer, *To Know As We Are Known* (Harper and Row: New York, 1983), 29.

4. *Ibid.*, 26.

5. *Ibid.*, 9.

6. *Ibid.*, 27.

7. Rorty, *op. cit.*, 333–35.

8. *Ibid.*, 170.

9. Palmer, *op. cit.*, 53.

10. *Ibid.*, 32–33.

11. Rorty, *op. cit.*, 174, (emphasis mine).

12. Palmer, *op. cit.*, 26.

13. Rorty, *op. cit.*, 318.

14. *Ibid.*

15. *Ibid.*

16. Palmer, *op. cit.*, 27–29.

17. "Remarks on Spencer's Definition of Mind as Correspondence," *The Journal of Speculative Philosophy,* 12 (1878), 1–18.

18. The entire passage is worth quoting: "Pretend what we may, the whole man within us is at work when we form our philosophical opinions. Intellect, will, taste, and passion co-operate just as they do in practical affairs; and lucky it is if the passion be not something as petty as a love of personal conquest over the philosopher across the way." And from the same essay, "If we survey the field of history and ask what feature all great periods of revival, of expansion of the human mind display in common, we shall find, I think, simply this: that each and all of them have said to the human being, 'The inmost nature of reality is congenial to powers which you possess.'" William James, "The Sentiment of Rationality," in John J. McDermott, ed., *The Writings of William James* (University of Chicago Press: Chicago and London, 1977), 334; 331.

19. James was, in my judgment, the most trenchant critic of positivist epistemology, but he was only one of several such dissenters from what was fast becoming the epistemological orthodoxy of his day. See, for example, James Kloppenberg's analysis of the four intellectuals who, along with James and Dewey, sought to develop, in Kloppenberg's terms, an epistemology of the *via media*. The four are Wilhelm Dilthey (1833–1900), whose father and grandfather were Calvinist ministers; Thomas Hill Green (1836–1882), whose father was also a clergyman; Henry Sidgwick (1838–1900), another clergyman's son who, along with Green, was among the founders of the Free Christian Union; and Alfred Fouille (1838–1912), whose goal was "to establish philosophy as the fusion of what is true in science, accompanied by an awareness of its limits, and what is true in religion, the experience of something beyond." Kloppenberg, *Uncertain Victory: Social Democracy and Progressivism in European and American Thought, 1870–1920* (Oxford University Press: Oxford and New York, 1986), 26–46; 36. For consideration of an exclusively American set of thinkers who dissented in various ways, during this same period, from positivism—Charles Peirce, James Mark Baldwin, Edward A. Ross, G. Stanley Hall, and Josiah Royce—see R. Jackson Wilson, *In Quest of Community: Social Philosophy in the United States: 1860–1920* (Oxford University Press: London and New York, 1968).

20. Palmer, *op. cit.,* 3–4.

21. Richard J. Bernstein, "Pragmatism, Pluralism, and the Healing of Wounds," *Proceedings and Addresses of the American Philosophical Association* 63 (3), 9.

22. *Ibid.* Peirce quoted by Bernstein.

23. Thomas Hobbes, *Leviathan* (Penguin Books: New York, 1981), 186–87.

24. Descartes, *Discourse on the Method,* in Elizabeth Anscombe and Peter Geech, eds., *Descartes: Philosophical Writings* (Bobbs-Merrill: Indianapolis, 1971), 19.

25. Jeffrey Stout, *The Flight from Authority* (University of Notre Dame Press: Notre Dame, 1981), 235, 250, and elsewhere throughout; Stephen Toulmin, "The Recovery of Practical Philosophy," *American Scholar* (Summer, 1988), 341–43.

26. Palmer, *op. cit.,* 26.

27. Rorty, *op. cit.,* 335.

28. The best account of the shift from Culture to cultures is George W. Stocking, Jr., "Matthew Arnold, E. B. Tylor, and the Uses of Invention," in George W. Stocking, Jr., *Race, Culture, and Evolution* (University of Chicago Press: Chicago, 1982), 69–90. Cf. also Stocking, *Victorian Anthropology* (The Free Press: New York, 1987), 302–30, and Clifford Geertz, "Thick Description: Toward an Interpretive Theory of Culture," in Clifford Geertz, *The Interpretation of Cultures* (Basic Books: New York, 1973), 4–5.

29. John Dewey, *The Public and Its Problems* (Swallow Press: Chicago, 1954), 143–84.

30. Rorty, *op. cit.*, 385.

31. R. S. Peters, *Ethics and Education* (George Allen and Unwin: London, 1968), 51.

32. Jeffrey Stout, *Ethics after Babel: The Languages of Morals and Their Discontents* (Beacon Press: Boston, 1988), 54.

33. Palmer, *op. cit.*, 69.

34. Michael Ignatieff, *The Needs of Strangers* (The Viking Press: New York, 1985), 138–39.

35. Stout, *Ethics after Babel*, 220–42, esp. 229.

36. Jeremy Waldron, "Particular Values and Critical Morality," *California Law Review* (77:553), 582.

37. Ignatieff, *The Needs of Strangers*, 139.

38. Gary B. Nash, "The Social Evolution of Preindustrial American Cities, 1700–1820: Reflections and New Directions," *Journal of Urban History*, 13 (February, 1987), 119, 133. I thank my colleague David Paul Nord for first drawing my attention to Nash's analysis.

39. Tonnies and Weber were part of a constellation of thinkers, including Ernst Troeltsch, Georg Simmel, and Georg Lukacs, for whom the terms *Gemeinschaft* and *Gesellschaft* were not only sociological categories but also terms with which they charted "the shift from a religious to a social framework of meaning. . . . To explain how man's social fate had replaced his religious fate was one of the chief ambitions underlying their work and remains a powerful, though seldom acknowledged, source of its enduring interest." Harry Liebersohn, *Fate and Utopia in German Sociology, 1870–1923* (Massachusetts Institute of Technology Press: Cambridge, 1988), 10.

40. Liebersohn points out that Tonnies was uncertain "whether *Gemeinschaft* referred to an actual historical example or to an abstract model more or less approximated by empirical social orders." I need also to stress that the German word was originally more restricted in its use than the English word *community*. The latter term *either* can refer to an *involuntary* social grouping like a network of families "bound together by a unity of wills and creating cooperation prior to its members' conscious choice [*Gemeinschaft*]," *or* can, more often, refer to *voluntary* "ethnic or religious groups, whose members are free to join or leave." Liebersohn, *Fate and Utopia*, 7. Clearly, academic communities are voluntary, but they are bound together by, among other things, a unity of purpose—the discovery of knowledge and truth.

3

Spirited Inquiry

I

All communities of higher learning are formed in large part by an ethos or spirit of inquiry. Indeed, all higher learning depends not simply upon the possession of certain cognitive skills but also upon the possession of moral dispositions or virtues that enable inquiry to proceed. Academies, if they are to flourish over the long run, must therefore cultivate and sustain in their members those virtues that are required for the kind of learning they hope to promote. Taken together, these virtues constitute the ethos of inquiry.

As epistemologies differ, however, so too do spirits of inquiry. I have argued that the Weberian ethos, connected as it is to a purely instrumental view of reason, exhibits its own characteristic set of motives (mastery, manipulation, and control) and virtues (clarity, honesty, diligence, dedication, and devotion to a rigorous regimen of disciplinary procedures). By contrast, communitarian epistemologies necessarily favor virtues that are less matters of purely personal integrity and more interpersonal or social in character. For communitarians, the pursuit of truth is linked inextricably to care taken with the lives and the thoughts of others. Though Weber banished charity and friendship from his conception of the academy, virtues such as these have constituted the spirit of inquiry for most of Western history. These virtues have, moreover, been spiritual in at least the strictly historical sense that they arose initially within communities that were self-consciously religious in character.

In this chapter, I propose to redescribe the present-day academy by examining the sense in which and the extent to which the conduct of academic life still depends upon such spiritual virtues as humility, faith, self-sacrifice, and charity. I offer this critical redescription as a corrective to the Weberian account of academic life, as an answer to Bok and others who are concerned about the ethical dimension of higher learning but who seem uncertain about where properly to locate the ethical within the academy, and as an effort to enrich current, communitarian accounts of learning. First, I shall mention briefly some historical warrants for and some cultural implications of linking spiritual virtues to learning and teaching. Then I shall demonstrate how and why certain spiritual virtues are indispensable to learning and teaching within the present-day academy. Finally, I shall develop briefly a conception of the academic vocation that views the self-conscious cultivation of a spiritually informed ethos of inquiry as a major aim of higher education.

II

The German Catholic philosopher Josef Pieper reminds us, in his little book *Scholasticism,* that the Platonic Academy was "a *thiasos,* a religious association assembling for regular sacrificial worship."[1] That academy was closed, after it had existed in Athens for nine hundred years, by the Christian emperor Justinian in 529 A.D. For the next thousand years, European philosophy, indeed most higher learning of any sort, took place in the cloistered environments provided by the church. Pieper suggests that the medieval period came to a close about the time in the fourteenth century that William of Ockham "fled from the Minorite cloister to the German imperial court [and] philosophy once more took up its residence in the larger 'breathing space' of the world."[2]

Few would dispute the central point here. Whether we look to the Platonic Academy or to the teachers of ancient Israel or to St. Augustine at Cassiciacum or to the medieval university or to Pico della Mirandola's disputatious Florence or even to the small colleges of early nineteenth-century America, we find learning flourishing in communities formed by the conscious practice of spiritual virtues. Over the course of the last century, the modern university has ceased, as we have seen, to attend to character formation, or it has imagined that such attention should be an "extracurricular" enterprise having little or nothing to do with knowledge. From this perspective, the current resurgence of the community question may be Western culture's way of awakening from a comparatively brief slumber induced or at least maintained by what Parker Palmer has called objectivism. If so, the "problem" is not to explain, much less to justify, the relationship between religion and higher learning: it is to account for how we could ever have lost sight of it.

This blindness to the relationship between spirituality and learning has been in part the fault of "enlightened" secular rationalism. David Hume, to take but one example of Enlightenment thinkers, concluded his *Inquiry Concerning the Principles of Morals* by contrasting the good human life, one that manifests Hume's own four moral principles, with an instance of the vicious human life, a kind of life based upon "superstition and false religion." Virtues for Hume were qualities of character that fall under four basic headings: those agreeable to oneself, those agreeable to others, those useful to oneself, and those useful to others. On this reckoning, monasticism, the form of life that had been the context for most of Western higher learning for a millennium, was for Hume rife with vice:

> Celibacy, fasting, penance, mortification, self-denial, humility, silence, solitude, and the whole train of monkish virtues—for what reason are they everywhere rejected by men of sense but because they serve to no manner and purpose; neither advance a man's fortune in the world, nor render him a more valuable member of society; neither qualify him for the entertainment of company, nor increase his power of self-enjoyment? We observe, on the contrary, that they cross all these desirable ends, stupefy the understanding and harden the heart, obscure the fancy and sour the temper. We justly, therefore, transfer them to the opposite column and place them in the catalogue of vices. . . .[3]

Hume understood very well that the Christianity of the monasteries was not merely a set of teachings but a way of life. And he here insisted, in castigating monasticism, that virtues like humility and self-sacrifice were inimical to learning, for they "stupefy the understanding and harden the heart." Like Max Weber over a century later, Hume, in the course of criticizing the superstitious aspects of the Christianity of his day, undermined some of the virtues, such as humility and charity, that make enlightened inquiry desirable and possible.

Blindness to the relationship between spirituality and higher learning is not, however, the result merely of the Enlightenment. The "superstition and false religion" that Hume assailed so mercilessly have persisted long after his critiques of them. At the end of the nineteenth century, at the very moment that the universities were consolidating the triumph of positivism, many of the religious were claiming that religion meant dogmatism based upon a peculiar reading of the Bible (Genesis as a geology text, for example). If the current ascendancy of the community question really does mark something of a recollection of the links between spirituality and learning, we might expect that the religious will rediscover the ethical dimension of their spirituality at the same time that some academicians rediscover the spiritual dimension of their ethos.

To speak in such abstract and exalted terms is to engage the language of hope, not optimism. For it is one thing to suggest that the life of learning will always be in some sense dependent upon the exercise of spiritual virtues in however attenuated a form, quite another to imagine that universities will return to the practice of those spiritual disciplines, such as prayer, that give those virtues meaning and strength. I do not therefore expect nor would I recommend any grand restructuring of the academy in the near future. Again I think that Parker Palmer is correct. He argues that the place to begin to counter the objectivist epistemology that still grips the academy is in individual classrooms where teachers, disciplining themselves first, create spaces "where obedience to truth is practiced." I shall now endeavor to demonstrate how higher learning, even today, entails the exercise, by students and teachers alike, of certain spiritual virtues.

III

The founder of the Platonic Academy wrote almost all of his philosophical works in dialogue form principally for the purpose of a similar demonstration of the interdependence of moral and intellectual virtues. The dialogue was and remains *the* vehicle best designed to dramatize the movement of inquiry as an act of life, involving characters in conversation, not intellects in isolation. The *Meno,* Plato's only dialogue on the subject of education, features a title character whose failures to learn are more frequently the results of flaws in his character than of lapses in his logic. Meno needs to change if he is to come to know the truth, to be "obedient to it" in Palmer's terms. Insofar as the truth comes to Meno, he does change—he becomes less arrogant, more self-disciplined, more courageous—not just in his ideas but in his way of living.

The questions that govern the movement of the *Meno*—Can virtue be taught? What is the relationship between knowledge and virtue? Is virtue a form of knowledge, or is it a gift from the gods?—are among the oldest in Western philosophy, and they are the same questions that underlie Derek Bok's worries about Harvard. Yes, the practices and the aims of education have changed many times from Plato's era to the modern university. Nevertheless, so long as the activities of teaching and learning involve communal questioning in search of the truth of matters, the exercise of virtues such as humility, faith, self-denial, and charity will be indispensable to higher education.

Consider first the virtue of humility. Much of what passes for laziness or the proverbial "lack of motivation" among today's students really involves a lack of humility, stemming in part from a lack of piety or respect for that aspect of God's ongoing creation that manifests itself in works of genius. I recently asked my students why they had not thought through a particular passage from St. Augustine on friendship and loss. I knew, because I had by that time grown to know these students very well, that they cared very much about the matters that Augustine was examining. I had not realized, however, that some of my students were easily convinced on the basis of a quick reading of the text, that Augustine was simply mistaken or overly agitated about these matters. Others complained that Augustine was unnecessarily obscure. All of them dismissed the passage in a peremptory fashion.

Current educational theory would suggest, in the face of these student comments, that I had failed properly to motivate them to want to learn about friendship and loss or that I had not managed to make Augustine accessible to them. I *had* probably failed in these ways. But my students could have overcome my failings had they been sufficiently humble; had they presumed that Augustine's apparent obscurity was *their* problem, not his; and had they presumed that his apparent inconsistencies or excesses were not really the careless errors they took them to be. Humility on this account does not mean uncritical acceptance: it means, in practical terms, the *presumption* of wisdom and authority *in the author*. Students and faculty today are far too often ready to believe that Kant was just, in a given passage, murky or that Aristotle was pointlessly repetitive or that Tolstoy was, in the battle scenes of *War and Peace,* needlessly verbose. Such quick, easy, and dismissive appraisals preclude the possibility of learning from these writers. Yes, some of these judgments may be warranted, but the practice of humility at least prevents them from being made summarily. *Some* degree of humility is a precondition for learning.

As is faith. James Gustafson has argued that "if the university is to be a fruitful location for exploring larger issues of life, perhaps we need to acknowledge, each of us as scholars, teachers, and students, that all our knowing involves 'faith,' human confidence in what we have received."[4] The point seems indisputable. We all rely upon the work and the thought of others, and we cannot possibly think well in an atmosphere of mistrust. Again, as in the case of humility, trusting the research and the theories of others does not mean accepting them uncritically. It means, as Gustafson has said, that we typically believe what we are questioning and at the same time question what we are believing. Faith then is a persistent beat in the rhythm of intellectual life. Without it, we would not be able to learn. All of us in some sense or another really do believe in order to understand.

At other moments in the life of learning, we must be prepared to *abandon* some of our most cherished beliefs. And we cannot do this unless we have to some extent cultivated the virtue of self-denial, the capacity first to risk and then to give ourselves up if necessary for the sake of the truth. The quest for knowledge of the truth, if it takes place within a context of communal conversation, involves the testing of our own opinions. And we must, of course, be willing to give up what we think we know for what is true, if genuine learning is to take place. At times, this will be easy, as when we learn that we were mistaken about some geographical detail or another. But much of our self-knowledge as well as our beliefs about what is truly good for us are not simply matters of what we know but matters of who we are. We thus often risk *ourselves* when we test our ideas.

Again, the link between our knowledge and our character is crucial here: to change our minds is, at times, to change our selves. Self-denial is just this disposition to surrender ourselves for the sake of the better opinion; wisdom is the discernment of when it is reasonable to do so. The "monkish" disciplines that cultivated self-denial (to return again to Hume) were to some extent a preparation for learning, a disposing of the soul toward an inner readiness to lose the self for the sake of the truth. The Italian Renaissance philosopher Pico della Mirandola argued that the conflicts that arise within a community of inquiry are "peculiar in that here it is a gain to lose. Consequently, anyone very weak can and should not only not disparage them [the struggles], but also seek them voluntarily, since the loser truly receives benefit and not injury from the winner, for through him the loser returns home richer. . . ."[5] I would prefer to say that truth is ideally the victor in these struggles. All participants lose, in the sense that they all surrender a part of themselves in the process of growing into the truth together.

Humility, faith, and self-denial: these practices neither exhaust the list of spiritual virtues that are indispensable to learning nor represent a list of *distinctively* Christian virtues. Indeed, the virtues I have thus far touched upon here did not originate from the example of Jesus of Nazareth. They arose instead from the practices and the teachings of the ancient Hebrews, a people whose deep and widely celebrated commitment to learning was and still is informed by an epistemology that is profoundly communal in character. To say, with Parker Palmer, that we must "recover from our spiritual tradition the models and methods of knowing as an act of love" is to direct us to the roots of that tradition in ancient Israel according to which knowledge and intimacy were one and the same.

As with the life of the spirit in general so too with the life of spirited inquiry: love or charity is the greatest of the virtues. To analyze fully the nature of charity and the occasions for its exercise within the academy would extend far beyond the scope of the present essay. Once again, some concrete illustrations of the fundamental importance of charity within the academy will have to suffice. And once again, I shall try to demonstrate, through the consideration of examples, that the exercise of charity has cognitive, not simply moral, dimensions.

Let me first consider briefly some aspects of my own study of history. I have in mind here criticism that I have received or that I have repeatedly leveled at myself regarding my thinking about, say, William James, a figure long dead. "You have really not done James full justice in your discussion of his religious views." Or again, "You really need to be more charitable to James in your analysis of his courtship and marriage." Notice that the vocabulary of moral and spiritual virtue— here justice and charity—easily insinuates itself into appraisals of thought as well as action. If I have grown to treat my colleagues and my students with justice and charity, am I more or less likely to treat historical subjects such as William James in the same manner? I am surely more likely to do so. And would such treatment increase or decrease the quality of my historical *thinking?* Again, I think that the exercise of charity toward my historical subjects is bound to make me a better historian: more cautious in appraisal, more sympathetic with human failings, less prone to stereotype and caricature. And insofar as this is so, the manner of teaching others to think historically ought to cultivate, at least through force of example, the virtue of charity.

As with history, so too with philosophy: charity both enriches and enlivens the quality of thought. To see how and why this is so, let us turn to another contemporary example, the recent work of a philosopher of religion, Jeffrey Stout. Stout's work is an important illustration of the operation of the virtue of charity for several reasons. First, his writing will help us to clarify the meaning of charity within the context of philosophical work. Second, the fact that Stout is an avowed nontheist will serve to remind us that though charity is indisputably a religious virtue, it can surely be present in persons who are not themselves religious. Finally, in the work of Stout that we will consider, he is writing about matters that pertain directly to the present discussion—the relationship between religious discourse and the secular academy.

Stout tells us in the introduction to *Ethics after Babel* that though he had considered "keeping the mention of other authors to a minimum," in the end he decided to engage the writings of others extensively for several reasons. He presents the two most important of them as follows: "I increasingly felt the need to test, clarify, and refine my views in extended dialogue with others who see the issues differently. And I discovered that much of what I wanted to say . . . could only be said in close readings of particular works." Thus, in Stout's own judgment, the quality of his own thinking improved in specific ways in the course of his conversation with other philosophers. Moreover, as I shall try now briefly to show, this philosophical improvement depended to some extent upon the charitable manner of that conversation.[6]

When Stout is considering the works of other philosophers, his charitable treatment of them evinces Luther's gloss upon the eighth commandment: "Put the best construction on everything." So, for example, when Stout is arguing with Richard Rorty, he strives at every point to construe Rorty's views in such a way that they represent cogent and incisive philosophical positions. He resists at almost every turn readings that would reduce Rorty's ideas to untenable dicta that could be easily assailed or summarily dismissed. "You get a charitable reading of

Rorty's pragmatism," Stout writes, "if you stress passages like [the one Stout has just quoted] over [Rorty's] 'pithy little formulae'. . . . I remain inclined toward a charitable reading of Rorty's writings on justice and truth. I therefore find it frustrating when Rorty relies excessively on pithy little formulae."[7]

Indeed, in his treatment of the thinkers he considers, Stout invariably works at interpreting passages that seem at first untenable until they become both more faithful to the larger and best intentions of these writers and philosophically more worthy of serious consideration. So, for example, when Rorty, in considering a hypothetical situation, asserts that one should *not* insist against one's torturers that there is something beyond the practices of their totalitarian society that condemns them, Stout finds the suggestion "false, on the first reading that occurs to me, even according to Rorty's own view." But instead of resting matters there with Rorty caught in an embarrassing inconsistency, Stout proceeds over the course of the next couple of pages to offer several alternative readings of Rorty's suggestion, some of them more and some of them less flattering to Rorty, all of them together advancing and deepening the understanding of the philosophical question at issue.[8]

Stout's charity is everywhere tempered by justice. He neither overlooks nor excuses culpable errors. So, for example, when he is considering the views of entire groups of people, past or present, his exercise of charity becomes at once more guarded and self-conscious. And it tends in these contexts to amount to a disposition to find ways of understanding, even though he cannot and should not share the erroneous views of others. When, on the one hand, he notes that some authors seem alternatively relativistic and nonrelativistic about moral matters, he insists that they "need not be guilty of contradiction, for we can take them, charitably, to be able to see the difference between justification and truth."[9] When, on the other hand, he excuses some of our ancestors for holding certain false opinions, he adds that we "shall not always want to be so charitable. . . . At times, we will be forced to explain a point of disagreement with our ancestors' moral beliefs not by saying they were justified in holding beliefs we now deem false but rather by saying that negligent reasoning, ideological rationalization, or wishful thinking led them to hold false beliefs."[10]

Charity is not the only one of the spiritual virtues considered thus far that Jeffrey Stout displays on almost every page of *Ethics after Babel*. Yet because he is an avowed nontheist, Stout would surely resist the notion that he owes his virtuous character to his present religious beliefs. Whereas for devout Christians and Jews the fear of the Lord is the beginning of wisdom, Stout's wisdom stems in part from a wholly secular piety that is "analogous to and even," he readily admits, "indebted to a central theme from the Reformed tradition."[11] Whereas Socrates's humility was related to the Apollonian religious tradition of the Delphic oracle, Stout's humility arises quite naturally "from observing human history and learning the facts of finitude."[12]

My argument, as I have thus far developed it, allows for the presence throughout human history of many pious and genuinely virtuous secularists like Jeffrey Stout. I have nowhere argued that there is some sort of absolute and necessary connection between religious belief and the virtues of humility, faith, self-sacrifice, and charity. I have, however, argued both for a historical connection between religious beliefs and these virtues and for an epistemological connection between the exercise of these virtues and the communal quest for knowledge and truth.

I should add now, before turning to a redescription of the academic vocation, a worry. I fear that most of our present-day academies as well as many academicians like Jeffrey Stout might be living off a kind of borrowed fund of moral capital. Although they may be able to draw continually upon these originally spiritual resources for the time being, Stout and other like-minded secularists may not be able either to replenish the fund or to transmit it intact to the next generation.

Why does Stout himself ignore altogether this worrisome possibility? He does note that we "live in a society where economic and other forces seem increasingly to produce people who lack the virtues needed to use their freedom well. . . ."[13] And he chooses to analyze the contemporary relationship between moral and religious language in part because he acknowledges what I have insisted upon here—the powerful historical connection between ethics and religion. He nevertheless underestimates the possibility that a decline in religious piety might be directly related to the decline in virtue he discerns, and he resists all attempts, such as the present one, to restore religiously informed practices and vocabularies to a prominent place within our public institutions.[14] This resistance does not derive from the mere fact that Stout is a nontheist, for he concedes that "it would indeed be fortunate for all of us, including atheistic fellow travelers, if . . . a form of biblical tradition essentially continuous with republican virtues began to flourish and enrich public life."[15] A brief effort to understand Stout's reasons for his suspicion of

religion will help us to understand further the cultural resistance that my
religiously informed redescription of the academic vocation must address and seek to overcome.

Stout opposes efforts to strengthen the public influence of religion in
part because he remains even today traumatized by the religious wars of
the seventeenth century, events that constitute the crucial episode in the
formation of the academic conscience of the West. Thus, for example,
Stout characterizes our society's recognition that the good life must
allow for our inability to agree upon any one model of the good life as
phronesis "forged in the religious strife of early modern Europe."[16] He
argues that theology has lost credibility among intellectuals largely because it "was unable to provide a vocabulary for debating and deciding
matters without resort to violence." And he often thinks of contemporary religion in terms of Belfast and Beirut, Teheran and Lynchburg,
places that give him "ample reasons for concern."[17]

I have already indicated part of my trouble with this line of argument.
Stout's sense of history from early modern Europe through most of the
twentieth century is highly tendentious at best. I do not think he would
accept my mention of Stalin, Mao, and Pol Pot, or of the gross ideological terrors inflicted upon huge populations by wholly secular but altogether autocratic regimes, left and right, as prima facie arguments
against secularism per se. They would be at best facts that warrant
resistance to particular kinds of secular ideologies and leaders. So, to be
charitable to Stout, we must look for the sources of his resistance to
religion in places other than his highly selective recollection of the past.

Stout reveals one of these sources in the following recommendation:
"Until theism proves able to gather a reasonably broad rational consensus around a specific conception of the good, an eventuality that now
seems remote, we probably should not follow advice like [Basil] Mitch-
ell's [to revive certain theological presuppositions]. The risks of reviving religious conflict like that of early modern Europe are too great."[18]
Remove the notion that theism should seek to achieve consensus about
the good, and the spectre of reviving religious conflict largely disappears. Suppose instead that I am correct: suppose that theism has been
and will continue to be responsible for cultivating and sustaining the
very virtues *that make productive study of and conversation among rival
conceptions of the good possible.* To the extent that this is true, the risks
of *weakening* the great religious traditions are too great. I can agree with
Stout that, in view of the traumatic religious conflicts that he remembers

so well, religion needs Enlightenment. To the extent that my analysis is correct, however, he should agree with me and against Hume that Enlightenment needs religion.

Another source of Stout's underestimation of the importance of religious virtues is the eclectic and hyperrational aspect of his own ethics, a strain that manifests itself most vividly in his penchant for what he calls *bricolage.* By *bricolage,* Stout means the creative synthesis of vocabularies and practices borrowed from different, sometimes competing, moral and religious traditions into an ethical discourse that is flexible enough to meet emergencies and surprises yet steady, humane, and principled enough to provide for human flourishing. I agree with him when he concludes his book by insisting that "the intellectual task of every generation . . . involves moral *bricolage.*" [19] Indeed, I intend the present book as my small contribution to that task.

Individuals, as Stout has shown us through precept and example, can practice *bricolage* readily and with impressive measures of success, but *bricolage* works less well—much more slowly for one thing—as a program for institutional reform or evolution. I may admire, learn from, and easily adopt Hindu dietary practices, absorbing them with only minor adjustments into my own stock of established practices and beliefs. But I cannot imagine that these practices could in the same ready manner be adopted on a mass scale within the United States. Peoples cannot add and subtract practices and virtues as they add and subtract ingredients in a recipe. In other words, you can change the inventory, even the configuration, of your beliefs much more easily than you can the configuration of institutional practices. The more deeply Hindu dietary practices are embedded within a system of religious observations and beliefs, the less likely that we can extract them for use as building blocks for our own polycultural *bricolage.*

In what I judge to be his more typical and better moments, Stout seems to realize all of this. He often reminds his reader that morals are much more a matter of feelings, attitudes, inclinations, and character than they are a matter of some thinly described rational deliberation, even presumably a deliberation informed by an eclectic set of beliefs. And he does argue that we need "the virtues required to live out our lives well from beginning to end and to *leave the next generation with a network of practices and institutions worth inheriting and continuing.*" [20] On the basis of his writing, I have little doubt that Stout himself possesses the requisite virtues, and I would guess that he can and does transmit these to the next generation if only through force of example. I do wonder, however, what devices, such as stories, rituals, practices, and other forms of institutional support, Stout has in mind for the transmission of the virtues he exemplifies to the next generation of Americans who are already, in his judgment, less virtuous than the previous one. The four spiritual virtues I have sketched out here have been nurtured and sustained over hundreds of years in part by the religious affection of piety. I therefore very much doubt whether they can be sustained over the course of several more generations absent the affections, practices, and institutions as well as the network of beliefs that gave rise to them originally. Stout can be comparatively complacent about this matter, in part because, as I have suggested, he has a sometimes overweening confidence in *bricolage.*

Consider once again, however, the spiritual virtue of humility. Stout's humility is related in part to his own "secular piety" and in part to his "observing human history and learning the facts of finitude." When compared, however, to the piety of a Socrates, a philosopher whom Stout admires deeply, or of a James Gustafson, a contemporary Christian ethicist whom Stout holds in very high esteem, Stout's secular piety does not seem particularly robust. It consists of his feelings of "wonder, awe, and even gratitude . . . for the powers that bear down upon us, for the majestic setting of our planet and its cosmos, and for the marvelous company we keep here."[21] One wonders how such feelings first arose in Stout and how he came to construe and appreciate the world in just this way. It cannot be the case that *simply* to behold the world and to contemplate the facts of finitude and human history invariably lead to these affections and thence to the virtue of piety. If these impressions were enough to instill piety within the human soul, virtue would prosper everywhere, and education as character formation would be a comparatively easy task.

On the contrary, however, some human beings are *first* formed in such a way that they become disposed to respond in a pious manner to the wonders of the world and human history and thence to practice humility. In Socrates's case, according to Plato's account in the *Apology,* this disposition arose in the course of a lifetime of pious struggle to obey the injunctions of the oracle at Delphi. The inscriptions on the wall of the temple of that oracle convey very well the spiritual virtues that it favored: "Know thyself; Nothing in excess; Curb thy spirit; Observe the limit; Hate hubris; Bow before the divine; Fear authority; Glory not in strength."[22] Thus Socrates tells his judges that the entire manner and purpose of his life were shaped by the worship of Apollo, who had ordered him "to lead the philosophic life examining myself and others."[23]

James Gustafson's Christian sense of piety is informed by an especially rich religious tradition extending from St. Augustine through John Calvin and Friedrich Schleiermacher to the present. Gustafson strenuously maintains that "morality and religion are, for those of religious consciousness, inextricably intertwined."[24] And for him the constitution of religious consciousness just is piety, meaning an "attitude of reverence, awe and respect . . . evoked by a powerful God who is the ultimate condition of possibility for human action and the ordering of life. . . ."[25] Stout complains that the God who evokes Gustafson's reverence is too bleak and severe a deity to "seem worthy of worship." He nevertheless shows a keen appreciation for other aspects of Gustafson's piety, especially for its "cognitive commitments" and its basis within "the context of a religious community, with its first-order religious language, its liturgies and symbols, and its procedures for transmitting a heritage."[26] When I say that Stout's secular piety, by comparison to the religious piety of Socrates and Gustafson, does not seem terribly robust, I mean that it lacks anchorage within just these kinds of communal practices and is hence not likely to be readily transmitted over time. Insofar as the spiritual virtues, such as humility, are strengthened by religious affections, their continued vitality would seem to be in some jeopardy under wholly secular auspices.

IV

This concern about the long-term vitality of the spiritual virtues brings me directly to the need for a redescription of the academic vocation as a calling informed by a sense of piety that is minimally Stoutian and maximally Gustafsonian. It was, of course, the vocabulary of Gustafson's variety of Protestantism that Max Weber transmuted during the course of his description of the academic calling in "Wissenschaft als Beruf." And it was this same Reformed tradition that led directly to Stout's version of secular piety with its feelings of awe toward, wonder at, and gratitude for powers that are not of our own making but that bear down steadily upon us.

As I have indicated, any compelling reconception of the academic calling will have to reckon seriously with Weber in part by recovering some of the more venerable notions of the nature and purposes of academic inquiry that his celebrated address so thoroughly and effectively undermined or ignored. To imbue the academic calling with secular or religious piety is already to change its Weberian character by redirecting its moral trajectory. For Weber, the point of academic life was *making* knowledge; under the present reconception, it is *seeking* the truth of matters. Instead of Weberian *mastery* of the world through calculation and control, academics ought primarily to seek understanding of the world through communal inquiry. This latter endeavor follows quite naturally from the affections of awe, wonder, and gratitude that together constitute piety. Finally, the means-end rationality that defined the academic mind for Weber must be absorbed into a far more capacious epistemology that views qualities of character, mind, and spirit as integrally related to one another.

Under this description, the principal task of academicians will not be to enable students to master life technically but to enable them to achieve a kind of academic excellence that harkens back in some respects to the Platonic Academy. That model of excellence, as we have seen, fully integrated moral and intellectual virtue. Leon Kass has cast this same objective in a more contemporary idiom by saying that colleges and universities ought to provide education "in and for thoughtfulness." The word *thoughtfulness* conveys, as Kass has noted, both the notion of being filled with reflections about important matters of human concern and the notion of being considerate of others. The same double meaning applies to the corresponding vice: to be thoughtless is to be both foolish and inconsiderate. My analysis has, I hope, persuasively deepened Kass's insight here. For I have been suggesting that one cannot be truly thoughtful in either of the two senses Kass has specified without being thoughtful in the other as well.[27]

This reorientation of academic life entails at least three radical revisions of the Weberian conception of the academic calling. First, teaching, not *Wissenschaft,* becomes the activity in terms of which all others—publication, collegiality, research, consultation, advising—are to be understood, interpreted, and appraised. Second, the cultivation of those spiritual virtues that make genuine teaching and learning possible becomes a vitally important aspect of pedagogy. Finally, both charity and *philia,* the loves that Weber banished from the academy, become once again central to its self-conception and to its overall mission in the world.

To maintain that teaching becomes *the* activity in terms of which all the others are to be understood is very different from saying merely that teaching should be more important than each of the other two members of the proverbial academic trinity—research, teaching, and collegiality. The former claim represents a conceptual shift, the latter a minor rearrangement of established priorities. So, for example, to construe writing as a fundamentally pedagogical act means, among other things, that the scholarly monograph becomes but one of several genres of writing honored by the academic community. General rhetorical and pedagogical principles, not simply the more narrowly defined disciplinary conventions, provide the standards by which written work is assessed. We could, under this dispensation, eventually come to see a day when Stephen J. Gould would be promoted as much on the basis of his splendid popularized (in the best sense of that term) essays, such as those that are collected in works like *The Panda's Thumb,* as on the basis of his highly technical and specialized monographs on aspects of evolutionary theory.

Under this description, the question of how to weigh publication relative to teaching in evaluating a colleague simply cannot arise. Instead, one might ask whether or not a given colleague has achieved a desirable balance between written and oral modes of pedagogy. And one might insist that all academicians display as keen and considerate a sense of their audiences, both inside and outside their classrooms, as they do of their subject matters. Clarity about whom one is writing to and for will come to be as important as clarity about what one is writing about. Again, the warrant for releasing academicians from the *exclusive* dominance exerted upon them by their respective professional guilds is the replacement of *Wissenschaft* as the informing purpose of the academic calling by the more encompassing aim of educating a variety of publics in and for thoughtfulness.

Reconceiving the academic vocation in this manner involves, of course, retrieving some of the ideas that were part of the German tradition of *Bildung* that Weber was rejecting, but it also entails revivifying conceptions of the life of learning that were for millennia embedded in religious communities. The idea that teaching ought to be the activity in terms of which all academic pursuits should be interpreted and valued was, for example, very dear to the heart of monastics like Bernard of Clairvaux. "There are many," St. Bernard wrote over seven hundred years ago, "who seek knowledge for the sake of knowledge: that is curiosity. There are others who desire to know in order that they may themselves be known: that is vanity. Others seek knowledge in order to sell it: that is dishonorable. But there are some who seek knowledge in order to edify others: that is love [*caritas*]. . . ."[28]

Though this way of writing might seem to readers of the present time like a word from a vanished world, I have tried to demonstrate that the connection drawn by Bernard between edification and charity resonates with certain contemporary cultural preoccupations. From secular thinkers like Rorty, we have seen renewed emphasis upon edification as the aim of philosophy, broadly understood; from religious thinkers like Palmer, we have seen accounts of knowing as a kind of loving. From both secular and religious thinkers, we have seen a recent resurgence of interest in communitarian epistemologies. These contemporary movements support the second radical revision of Weber's understanding of the academic vocation: the conception of academics as persons who cultivate in themselves and in their students the spiritual virtues that make genuine learning possible.

To "teach" these virtues means first to exemplify them, second to order life in the classroom and throughout the academic community in such a way that their exercise is seen and felt as an essential aspect of inquiry. Jeffrey Stout has served us here as a model of considerate and judicious appraisal of the thoughts of others. And when he celebrates the ideal of human beings "caught up in a conversation that leads to unexpected self-understanding," he has in passing noted one of the many ways in which classroom activity can achieve cognitive purposes through the cultivation of spiritual virtues.[29] The teacher must, in other words, submit herself to the disciplines and the arts of inquiry that enable communities to grow together into new understandings. This will be no easy task, because the temptations to self-promotion will recur in numerous guises throughout the course of any teaching career. Still, modeling the spirited conversation in the classroom is the surest way to shape the direction and enhance the quality of each student's thought processes.

Cardinal Newman certainly made these points, as he made so many others, more eloquently than anyone else before or since.

The personal influence of the teacher is able in some sort to dispense with an academical system, but that system cannot in any sort dispense with personal influence. With influence there is life, without it there is none; if influence is deprived of its due position, it will not by those means be got rid of, it will only break out irregularly, dangerously. An academical system without the personal influence of teachers upon pupils is an arctic winter; it will create an ice-bound, petrified, cast-iron University and nothing else.[30]

It is an eerie coincidence perhaps that Weber's last works were filled with similar images of cold, darkening loneliness: the future of German politics in the immediate aftermath of World War I he called a "polar night of icy darkness"; the modern university in the twentieth century, an outpost of exiles, not unlike the ancient Hebrews, inquiring of and in the night; the dwelling place of the "specialists without spirit," an iron cage of their own making.[31]

But these images should not really surprise us, for, as we have seen, Weber quite explicitly banished all forms of love from the academy as well as from other realms of life such as the state and the economy that were governed purely by means-end rationality. I have already examined how and why the greatest of the spiritual virtues, charity, is essential to the process of communal inquiry. But charity is not the only form of love that belongs properly and centrally to the life of learning. "Thoughtfulness, in both senses, is," as Kass notes, "the core of the best friendships."[32] I should like now to conclude my redescription of the academic vocation by addressing more fully the suggestion that I made at the close of Chapter I. I will argue that academies at their best can and should become communities where the pleasures of friendship and the rigors of work are united.

Many students and faculty sense this possibility at the level of their most rudimentary impressions. Perhaps most of the students who remain deeply attached to their alma mater do so not so much out of gratitude for the range of cognitive abilities they acquired as out of appreciation for the quality and endurance of the friendships they formed. Faculty speak regularly and solemnly about the critical importance of "collegiality," a quality that seems unfortunately as crucial to possess as it is impossible to define. Most faculty members are, however, deeply suspicious of friendships with students, for they instantly reduce all such relationships between persons unequal to one another in some respect to a kind of chumminess that is demeaning to both parties.

On this matter, the students' sentiments are a surer source of insight into the character of academic community than are the faculty's thoughts. We need, however, Aristotle's rich conception of *philia* to render the thinking that accompanies the students' feelings articulate and precise. For Aristotle, friendship or *philia* was the crowning virtue of the good life for human beings, "for without friends no one would choose to live, though he had all other goods."[33] *Philia* was, moreover, an elastic concept that embraced an enormous range of human relationships, including those of rulers and ruled, parents and children, teachers and students, citizens and citizens. In other words, friendship was, for Aristotle, a much broader and richer category than our contemporary notion. Moreover, once Aristotle began to distinguish carefully the various kinds of friendship, he could and did capture the singular strengths and limitations of, to give two examples, friendships among those who are unequal with respect to age, experience, and training, and friendships among those who constitute together a large intentional community. On Aristotle's account, friendships between teachers and students as well as friendships among the many academics at, say, UCLA would be both possible and desirable.

Of the several kinds of friendship, the highest and best was the friendship of virtuous human beings, equal to one another, who live a life together "sharing in discussion and thought." The deepest intimacy between human beings arose in this process of conversation, because, for Aristotle, human beings were most fully and truly themselves when they were thinking together. And so for him, as for so many of the other writers we have mentioned or studied, thinking and speaking together were expressions of a kind of love.[34]

We need not enter here into all of the important discriminations that would be required for a complete analysis of the various kinds of friendship that can and should exist in a flourishing academy at any given time. We can, however, surmise, on the basis of what we have seen regarding the cognitive significance of the spiritual virtues, that without the virtue of friendship, academic life threatens to become a mere technological project. The converse also seems to be the case. Once the academy is conceived to be an enterprise governed exclusively by the practice of means-end rationality, once the academic vocation is construed exclusively in terms of *Wissenschaft,* the virtue of friendship will soon disappear from any account of those virtues essential to its highest aspirations.

These contrasts cannot be more stark. For Weber and others, making knowledge is a solitary and lonely, often a competitive, process. Human beings' wishing one another well, a crucial aspect of any community of friends, may in fact be linked from time to time to the process of making knowledge, but the connection is not an essential one. By contrast, just as and just because, for Aristotle, practical wisdom and the moral virtues mutually implicate one another, so too thinking well and living well are mutually implicated at the conceptual level, in the very definition of human excellence. And because the highest form of friendship is a friendship between virtuous human beings, *philia* and inquiry, love and the pursuit of truth, enrich one another. It is no wonder that so often the most durable of the friendships that human beings form arise in the context of learning together.

The literary critic Wayne Booth has sought to extend the Aristotelian notion of friendship to include as well a reader's relationship to the implied author of a text.[35] Insofar as this project succeeds—and I believe that it does succeed to a great extent—we can extend the boundaries of the academy to include the living and the dead, those who speak to us face to face and those who address us from across the centuries through the printed word. Booth recognizes the limitations of efforts to construe books as friends, but he nevertheless makes a persuasive case for his more general claim that we are formed to a great extent by the "company we keep." By inviting us to consider implied authors as friends he further reinforces the cognitive importance of spiritual virtues such as humility and charity, both of which are suggested by Booth's golden rule of hermeneutics, "Read as you would have others read you; listen as you would have others listen to you."[36] To construe the academy contra Weber as a community of friends is paradoxically to stress at one and the same time loyalty to particular places where human beings can inquire together over long periods of time and the need for a company of very diverse books from lands remote in space and time whose authors constitute, at least potentially, the loved ones we hold in common as part of our intellectual tradition.

We have seen in this chapter how and why the spiritual virtues are indispensable even today to academic inquiry and in any case how and why they should be central to alternative conceptions of the academic vocation. We are left simply to wonder whether any cultural resources other than religious ones can counter the technological tendencies within the academy that Weber both analyzed and advanced. We are also left to wonder about many practical matters, and we shall turn to these in the next chapter.

Notes

1. Josef Pieper, *Scholasticism* (Pantheon: New York, 1960), 155.
2. *Ibid.*
3. David Hume, *An Inquiry Concerning the Principles of Morals* (Bobbs-Merrill: Indianapolis, 1976), 91.
4. James Gustafson, "Human Confidence and Rational Activity," *Cresset* (September, 1988), 17.
5. Pico della Mirandola, "On the Dignity of Man," trans. Charles Glenn Wallis, in *On the Dignity of Man and Other Works* (Bobbs-Merrill: Indianapolis, 1981), 20.
6. Jeffrey Stout, *Ethics after Babel: The Languages of Morals and Their Discontents* (Beacon Press: Boston, 1988), xi.
7. *Ibid.*, 246.
8. *Ibid.*, 259–60.
9. *Ibid.*, 30.
10. *Ibid.*, 31.
11. *Ibid.*, 182.
12. *Ibid.*, 25.
13. *Ibid.*, 232.
14. *Ibid.*, 286.
15. *Ibid.*, 223.
16. *Ibid.*, 238.
17. *Ibid.*, 223.
18. *Ibid.*, 222–23.
19. *Ibid.*, 292.
20. *Ibid.*, 291 (emphasis mine).
21. *Ibid.*, 181.
22. C. D. C. Reeve, *Socrates in the Apology* (Hackett: Indianapolis and Cambridge, 1989), 30.
23. Socrates in the *Apology* quoted by Reeve, *op. cit.*, 71.
24. James Gustafson, *Ethics from a Theocentric Perspective,* vol. I (University of Chicago Press: Chicago, 1981), 167.
25. *Ibid.*, 164.
26. Gustafson quoted by Stout, *Ethics after Babel,* 194.
27. Leon Kass, "The Aims of Liberal Education," unpublished address delivered in Rockefeller Chapel, the University of Chicago, September 25, 1981.
28. St. Bernard of Clairvaux quoted by Pieper, *Scholasticism,* 89.

29. Stout, *Ethics after Babel,* 194.

30. John Henry Cardinal Newman, *University Sketches* (The Walter Scott Publishing Company: London and New York, 1902), 73.

31. Max Weber, "Politics as a Vocation," in H. H. Gerth and C. Wright Mills, trans. and eds., *From Max Weber: Essays in Sociology* (Oxford University Press: New York, 1977), 128; "Science as a Vocation," *op. cit.,* 156; *The Protestant Ethic and the Spirit of Capitalism,* trans. Talcott Parsons (Charles Scribner's Sons: New York, 1958), 181–82.

32. Kass, "The Aims of Liberal Education," 22.

33. Aristotle, *The Nicomachean Ethics,* trans. W. D. Ross (Oxford University Press: Oxford and New York, 1986), book 8, part 1, 192.

34. *Ibid.,* book 9, part 9, 240–41.

35. Wayne Booth, *The Company We Keep: An Ethics of Fiction* (University of California Press: Berkeley, Los Angeles, London, 1988), 169–96.

36. *Ibid.,* 172–73.

4

Questions and Considerations

To insist, as I have, that conversation is central to the life of the mind and then to fail to act upon this claim would be at best a serious lapse in judgment. I have accordingly framed a series of questions that my friends and colleagues, all of them named in the Acknowledgments, have actually raised about the analysis and arguments I have thus far advanced. Most of these questions involve practical matters, and they arise from doubts about the desirability of some consequences of my general recommendations or about the feasibility of realizing any one of them. Other questions, however, pose difficulties for some of my basic assumptions. None of them invites an easy "answer"; I have therefore responded to all of them with a set of considerations designed to advance our thinking, not to settle the issues that they raise once and for all.

Question: However well intended and even persuasive the alternative account of the academic vocation might be, its effect is likely to be unfortunate. Will it not give aid and comfort to the mediocrities on all college and university faculties, since it will seem to warrant their lack of scholarly publication by legitimating all sorts of other activities as worthy of academic respect?

Considerations: The inadvertent promotion of mediocrity would indeed be unfortunate, but so too would be the acceptance of the implicit equation that the question draws between academic mediocrity and lack of scholarly publication. There may well be an empirical correlation between these two things, but there should not be, for that reason, a strong conceptual link presumed between them. The explanation for the often alleged statistical correlation between mediocrity and low scholarly "productivity" has less relation to the intrinsic connections between scholarship and teaching than to sloth, the vice that leads both to poor teaching and to a lack of publication.

It may be that the apprehension that gives rise to the present question involves the conflation of two sets of distinctions into one. One set is qualitative, the other generic; one embraces the excellent, the good, the mediocre, and the bad; the other embraces the academic monograph, the book review, the essay, the textbook, the critique of a colleague's manuscript, the written lecture, in brief all inscribed instances of pedagogy. Thus far, we have critically examined the tendency to privilege one form of teaching, the academic monograph, to the point that it is presumed good until proved bad, while all other written forms of teaching are presumed deficient by the highest academic standards until proved worthy of professional regard.

Let us now turn to another misapprehension that might well underlie the present question. Contrary to this misapprehension, the alternative account of the academic vocation developed in the preceding chapter in no way suggests that to write something or, for that matter, to hold forth in front of a class or to evoke vocalized noise in a classroom is to do something worthy of respect. It *should* not be necessary to insist upon the difference between doing something and doing something well, but at least some of the criticism of the sort suggested by the present question rests upon a failure to maintain this obvious distinction. The previous chapter did argue for construing the whole of the academic vocation as teaching and therefore for broadening the kinds of written endeavors that should be legitimately regarded as worthy of academic respect. But it nowhere suggests that academics ought to be praised, promoted, or otherwise rewarded simply for making any one of these efforts. On the contrary, making the efforts ought to be the minimal requirement for continued remuneration; succeeding in them, in the judgment of one's peers, ought to be the minimal requirement for tenure and promotion. Excellence of the kind described in the preceding chapter should be the primary, if not the sole, consideration informing all personnel decisions.

Question: Because teaching is far more difficult to evaluate than written work, how can anyone fairly and accurately promote and retain faculty simply on the basis of their teaching?

Considerations: Remember that the term *teaching,* as we have been using it here, does not refer to but one of several distinct tasks that academics perform. Instead, it captures the whole of what they do or should be doing. We should therefore include the evaluation of academics' written work as a part of the appraisal of their teaching. But let us turn directly to the matter of appraising those activities that have customarily fallen under the heading of teaching—preparing courses, lecturing, leading discussions, evaluating student work, tutoring, and so on. Do the alleged difficulties in appraisal arise from the nature of these activities themselves or from the unwillingness of institutions of higher learning to expend the time and energy necessary first to think these matters through carefully and then to initiate and sustain those practices that would make the fair and accurate assessment of teaching a routine activity within academic communities?

These are very difficult questions that defy glib and ready answers. Let us here begin to address them by demystifying matters a bit. Let us first note that a substantial portion of traditionally defined teaching activities, such as lectures, course syllabi, and evaluations of student work, is inscribed. In addition, mechanisms for course evaluations by students and peers have long been used at most colleges and universities. Finally, many other standard practices permit, even encourage, the appraisal of colleagues' teaching: departmental seminars, faculty workshops, videotaping of classes, and the like. In brief, the materials on the basis of which one might appraise teaching are often in abundant supply, and though pedagogy is an art, it is most definitely not a mystery.

Even so, if the present reconception of the academic vocation were seriously adopted in practice, colleges and universities would have to multiply and institutionalize occasions for appraisal, and this would be all to the good. In curricular terms, this might well mean the proliferation of staff-taught courses, joint endeavors that would provide natural, regular, and hence all the more comfortable opportunities for peer review and encouragement of pedagogy. On the co-curricular front, consider practices like the one sponsored by the English Department at my university called "Books and Coffee." Every week during the spring term teachers from the university and citizens from the surrounding community gather together to hear a faculty member deliver a forty-minute review of a book deemed worthy of public attention. Approximately twenty minutes of conversation follows. Some faculty have turned these lectures into review essays and published them. Others have been more informal. But all of them have faced and sought publicly to meet this specially challenging teaching situation involving a group of highly educated colleagues combined with a group of sometimes barely informed townspeople. Needless to say, informal but candid and extensive evaluations of faculty members' pedagogical virtues have invariably followed closely upon the conclusion of these endeavors.

Question: This kind of appraisal will lead directly to something like "character tests." Isn't this always a dangerous business in academia?

Considerations: To question these patterns of appraisal is warranted; to fear them is misguided, because such fears are largely based upon an erroneous distinction between character on the one hand and intellect on the other. According to the present account, we will appraise scholars' characters by examining the nature of their thought and action on the many occasions upon which they have either made their ideas public or provoked thoughtful discussion among others in a manner permitting us to study them. And it will not be possible, on this reckoning, to distinguish sharply between qualities of character and qualities of mind. A reviewer who tempers justice with charity just will be to that extent a better reviewer than one who is uncharitable or unjust. Those who take delight in repeatedly humiliating (to be sharply distinguished from occasionally humbling) students will be regarded as both morally foolish and intellectually arrogant.

Does not the principal danger in the matter of appraisal arise from the belief that, under the present system, academics are judged in a manner that bleaches their character traits from them and leaves only naked, shivering reasoners and their written remains to be examined and dissected? In other words, we already appraise character as perhaps the major consideration in awarding tenure and promotion, but we lack a refined vocabulary to do this, because we feel that, given our prior, albeit tacit, commitment to separate cognition from spiritual and moral virtue, we must pretend otherwise. The present proposals would permit us to drop the pretense and to be much more explicit and thoughtful about the range of characters that we most want or need within a given academic community at a given time in its history.

Question: Will applying these considerations turn out to be a hopelessly imprecise and therefore dangerous business in practice?

Considerations: Yes, the business of appointments, tenure, and promotion will be imprecise relative to arithmetic, but we should only expect it to be as precise as the subject matter warrants. It will be very important to have good judges, virtuous in the appropriate ways, making personnel decisions. No algorithm for making these judgments currently exists, and none could or should ever come into being. It will be important to consider the needs of a given community at a given time in its history, the quality of the teaching, the question of how to weigh the various expressions of pedagogy relative to one another, in sum the whole appraisal of character with an eye upon those virtues most needed by the community to advance its corporate task of education in and for thoughtfulness.

No set of procedures can guarantee that these judgments will be made well. We can reasonably hope, however, that the conversation that will necessarily take place in the search for justice and wisdom in these matters will be more centrally bound up with the kind of questions and considerations that appropriately animate a genuine intellectual community. We should acknowledge that the conversations might also be more protracted and strife-ridden than they are presently. Even so, it seems worthwhile to engage in protracted conflict over fundamental questions, especially when the general health of the community depends upon the outcome.

Question: Does not this whole way of thinking needlessly confuse the relationship between teaching and research?

Considerations: Consider the following anecdote about this relationship related by J. M. Cameron in his fine little book, *On the Idea of a University.* During the academic year 1965–66, the British University Grants Committee asked universities to find out from their senior faculty members "how their work was divided between preparation for undergraduate teaching, preparation for graduate teaching, and research." Upon hearing of this peculiar request, a writer for the *London Times* had the good wit to observe that the inquiry was rather like asking a sheep "how much of its time is devoted to growing wool and how much to turning itself into mutton."[1]

Unfortunately, the situation in U.S. universities today is, if anything, even less enlightened than that created by the British University Grants Committee in the 1960s. No question is as frequently or as futilely debated among faculty as the question of the relationship between teaching and research. This debate has been so sterile (it merely repeats itself in a thousand forms) because, as the preceding anecdote suggests, it is hopelessly misconceived. Asking about the relationship between research and good teaching is somewhat like asking about the relationship between being single and being a bachelor. All bachelors are single (as all good teachers are researchers), but not all single persons (we may think of women and children) are bachelors (not all researchers are good teachers). This exercise in elementary logic should go some distance toward clearing up the conceptual problem, but alas it does not. The institutional context that gives meaning to the vocabulary of teaching and research is extremely complex; discourse about teaching and research cannot therefore be entirely reduced to elementary logical distinctions.

In truth, the modern comprehensive university can no longer define, with either confidence or precision, those activities that were once deemed central to its mission—teaching and research. A professor of psychology has a private clinical practice. This clinical work is, from the psychology professor's point of view, research; from the physics professor's point of view, moonlighting; and from the provost's point of view, another troubling feature of academic life (unless, of course, the provost happens to be a clinical psychologist). From no one's point of view is the clinical work by itself scholarship, although many people use the terms *scholarship* and *research* interchangeably. Perhaps then the clinical work *becomes* scholarship when its results are published. Almost, but not quite. Under the present dispensation, this latter issue will be resolved in part on the basis of *where* the results are published.

Nor is the case of the professor of clinical psychology exceptional. The professor of drama directs plays. Are the performances that result from these endeavors the fruits of research, instances of scholarship, theatrical versions of publication (careful here; the performances are, after all, public, though perishable), displays of professional competence, evidences of good (or bad) teaching, or mere entertainments? Who can say? Who *should* say?

These problematic examples have been taken thus far from within what has traditionally been called the college of arts and sciences. But consider for a moment the professional schools and colleges. One consequence, perhaps the major consequence, of the proliferation of "professionalism" within the academy has been a bewildering profusion of meanings for terms like *teaching, research, scholarship,* and even, perhaps especially, *professionalism* itself. Is there a difference between consulting work and research in the various professions? If so, what is it? Is on-the-job training a form of teaching? What about off-the-job training? A CPA brilliantly settles the accounts of Bethlehem Steel, saving the corporation millions of tax dollars in the process. Now this same CPA becomes a professor of accounting, all the while retaining the Bethlehem account. What do we now call the professor's accounting work? Research? Continuing education? Community service? Moonlighting? A contribution to the profession?

The university has decided not to answer questions like the ones I have just posed in any uniform manner. Instead, it supports the academic expression of professional pluralism—departmentalism. Departments decide what constitutes adequate research, scholarship, teaching, and so forth, though there may be little or no agreement across departments, much less across colleges, about such matters. So a situation that is very confusing in theory is not quite so confusing in practice unless one seeks consistency and coherence in the university as a whole.

We need to dwell upon this matter extensively here, because so many of the questions raised about the redescription of the academic vocation that we are examining have impinged in one way or another upon the relationship between teaching and research. So we might ask whether this redescription actually brings some measure of clarity and order to an otherwise chaotic situation. We have placed teaching at the center of academic life. This means that many of the activities enumerated here will not be considered central to the purpose of a university, for instance, settling the accounts of Bethlehem Steel. In the process of reconceiving academic life, we have applied Occam's razor to some extent. We have conflated the three elements of the academic trinity—teaching, publication, and collegiality—into at most two. And much of what is currently understood by the term *collegiality* could easily be subsumed under teaching in the extended sense used here.

We need to remember, in any event, that the meaning of research, like the meaning of teaching, has changed before and is likely to change again. From the time of Herodotus and for most of Western history thereafter, it meant simply "inquiry." Indeed, if James Turner and Paul Bernard are correct, research, even for several years *after* German models of higher learning were imported to the United States during the last half of the nineteenth century, meant something like "looking up information independently, as an undergraduate is now said to 'do research' for a term paper."[2] But, as Turner, Bernard, and many other historians have argued, research soon came to mean what it still means to most people today, namely scholarship that *advances* knowledge of a subject matter within a *specialized* field of learning. One salutary impact of the burgeoning professional schools has been to reestablish the connection between disciplined learning and research on the one hand and human flourishing on the other, a connection that has been recurrently disavowed by liberal arts departments that extol the virtues of specialized knowledge "for its own sake."

The inclination of the present analysis is toward retrieval and reinvigoration of the most venerable meaning of the terms that once gave dignity and purpose to a university education. To construe research as inquiry is to bring it once again primarily within the larger domain of thoughtfulness, secondarily within the domain of specialized learning. This would not necessarily entail resistance to the modernist imperative of specialization. But it would require university teachers to render explicit the motives and the larger questions that inform their investigations, however specialized those investigations might be. Pseudo-questions about the relationship between teaching and research would be replaced by the genuine questions, such as, Why inquire? or What is the point or the worth of *this* inquiry? Keeping these latter questions alive would seem essential to the task of any university worth its name.

Question: If, as you have noted, most faculty publish very little, are you not addressing matters here that are perhaps interesting but relatively insignificant?

Considerations: We should not underestimate the number of faculty who, because they do not publish in prestigious scholarly journals, labor with a bad conscience. These often dedicated souls never wholly lose the inner conviction, instilled at every turn in graduate school, that scholarly publication just is "their own work," and that nothing else really matters. Rhetoric is at wide variance with reality here, perhaps especially among administrators who characterize their own universities as "teaching institutions" (again promoting the invidious distinction between teaching and research already noted) and then proceed to promote faculty primarily on the basis of scholarly publication. We should expect most faculty to write *more* than they do, because they should endeavor to teach larger and larger publics. The present redescription of the academic calling should be useful in this regard, because it enlarges the kinds of writing that ought to be considered forms of teaching and therefore worthy of appraisal as endeavors integral to the academic vocation. Even so, we should admit that there exists among the active and committed ranks of any university faculty a diversity of pedagogical talents, and we should seek discernment of these and then advocate concurrent institutional adjustments that mobilize them most effectively.

At most colleges and universities, the administration should recognize the existence of a least two such groups of differently gifted faculty and move instantly to reckon wisely and publicly with this fact. Faculty in the first group should continue to enjoy their privileges as teachers and academic citizens. If they prove to be excellent classroom teachers, they should be warmly rewarded for their work. They should not be expected to publish. But they should be expected to do more classroom teaching and more committee work than the faculty in the second group.

The second group should be expected to serve on committees, to engage in classroom teaching, and to publish. If they do all of these things well, they should be warmly rewarded also, no more and no less than the first group. But they should *not* be expected to spend as much time in the classroom or to serve on as many committees as the faculty in the first group. Indeed, their course assignments (note that this is *not* the same as their *teaching* ''loads'') should be reduced by at least one course per term, and their committee assignments should be half of what might fairly be expected of those in the first group. Finally, these faculty will be eligible for publication support funds that the university should have at its disposal. Two groups: two sets of overlapping criteria for tenure, promotion, and compensation. Divide and consider.

How should the two groups be identified? By self-selection. Let faculty assign themselves into one of the two groups during a period of one or two years. During that time departments should make explicit the procedures for evaluating peers in both groups. Faculty, in other words, should decide for themselves what constitutes good teaching in all of its forms within their own respective disciplines. These criteria will vary to some extent from department to department. Nevertheless, a university committee of faculty should review the departmental guidelines and their rationales to ensure that the university really is pursuing a *common* concern for teaching and learning as its constitutive activities. At the end of the self-selection period, the two groups should go forth with mutual respect and support. The variance in their gifts and preferences will have led to a corresponding variance in their communal functions. There should be no sense of second-class citizenship in either group.

Again, the major problem in this entire area of academic life stems not from the fact that most faculty do publish (a small fraction actually does so regularly) but from the guilty consciences of those who do not. This problem can be addressed only if we can manage to change the inner sense of the academic calling along some of the lines advanced previously. The institutional adjustments outlined here in response to the present question will be meaningless absent a new understanding of the purpose of academic life.

Question: Will the redescription of the academic vocation offered here, however well intended it might be, still result in the promotion of teaching *at the expense* of scholarship?

Considerations: Such a thing *may* result, but it *need* not and it *should* not. Good teachers love scholarship, honor it, and depend upon it in order to be good teachers. The point of the redescription offered here is not to diminish scholarship but to accept it as a form of teaching by recognizing that it has substantive human goods beyond itself at which it aims. Many of us college teachers wish that we could do more scholarship and that we were better at doing it than we are: these are noble aspirations. But these longings are very different from the debilitating sense that our calling is defined exclusively by scholarship "for its own sake." Again, the point here is to restore teaching to the premier place of dignity and honor that it once had but that it has lost over the course of the years, but there is *no* intention to do this by denigrating scholarship.

Consider the following analogy. The end of medicine is health. Without biomedical scholarship, we could not attain that end. But it would be absurd to argue that physicians ought to be trained primarily to do biomedical scholarship or that those physicians who attend exclusively to healing the sick are somehow not really doing "their own work." It would also be absurd to imagine that biomedical scholarship is best done "for its own sake." Some physicians would make poor biomedical scholars; some biomedical scholars would make poor physicians. Yet the two groups sometimes overlap and, when they do not, they depend upon one another in order honorably to achieve the end of medicine. Finally, *both* groups must do research.

So it is (roughly) with higher learning. Its end is thoughtfulness or wisdom, the health of the human soul. Without scholarship (one form of teaching), we could not attain this end. But we should not therefore suppose that *all* college teachers should be trained exclusively for scholarship or evaluated primarily upon the basis of their publication record. Some scholars are poor classroom teachers; some classroom teachers are poor scholars. But excellence in both forms of teaching depends upon excellence in research. This excellence depends upon other things as well, such as excellence in the arts of rhetoric and dialectic.

In accepting the Weberian description of the academic vocation, we have emphasized one of its aspects (scholarship) to the exclusion of all others, and we have sometimes acted as though the advancement of learning has no end beyond the advancement of learning. At its very worst, this conception of the academic vocation has legitimated the sneering jibe, "Those who can [do scholarship], do; those who can't, teach." Such a jibe about the practice of medicine would be inconceivable. That it *is* conceivable (and still circulated) within the academy demonstrates the need for a redescription of the academic vocation.

Question: Is not the vision of virtuous communities of inquiry hopelessly utopian after all? Could we really enlist the serious support of any institution that takes research (in the more conventional sense) to be a significant part of its central mission?

Consideration: This question about utopia arises from the avowed suspicion that spirited learning communities like the ones previously described could exist literally "no place." But communities of learning that do justifiably pride themselves upon the generation of the very highest and best thinking about important matters of human concern already aspire to something very like the vision set forth here. Let us consider three very different examples, two of them on the basis of their explicit programmatic statements, one on the basis of personal testimony.

First, let us examine a recent publication of the Hastings Center. On the occasion of the center's twentieth anniversary in June 1989, several speakers offered critical and sometimes conflicting presentations about the relations among ethics, human nature, and medical progress. In introducing the issue of the *Hastings Center Report* that included those presentations, the editor, Courtney Campbell, offered approvingly K. Danner Clouser's articulation of the spirit of rational inquiry as a summary statement of the aspirations of the center itself:

May we ever keep our work in perspective.
May we argue incessantly but without acrimony.
May our caring for each other outshine our refutations of each other.
May our cleverness never obscure our goals of justice and morality.
May the spirit of good will and fellowship always pervade our work together.[3]

We cannot be sure, of course, that these resolutions actually characterize the work of the Hastings Center. But we can be sure that our second example describes a group of scholars whose avowed intentions were realized in a book that itself enacts the very process of inquiry that it recommends. I refer here to the five scholars who collectively wrote *Habits of the Heart.* These academics quite self-consciously sought to practice the kind of spirited inquiry described in the preceding chapter. They met regularly to think through and converse about the questions and the evidence that they had gathered. They wrote the entire book together instead of parceling sections of it out piecemeal. And they repeatedly recognized the interdependence between the spiritual and the intellectual virtues in their common work. This interdependence applied not only to the relationships among the five scholars but also to the relationships between them and their subject(s):

> What we learned as a result of our study is a contribution toward our own self-understanding as well as to social self-understanding. It is impossible to draw a clear line between the cognitive and the ethical implications of our research, not because we cannot make an abstract distinction between the analysis of evidence and moral reasoning, but because in carrying out our research both are simultaneously operative. We cannot deny the moral relationship between ourselves and those we are studying without being untrue to both.[4]

Unfortunately this example of a community of spirited inquiry is still exceptional, one of the reasons perhaps that *Habits of the Heart* has gained so much controversial attention from both the academy and the general educated public. I suspect from experience, however, that the animation of a great deal of the learning that goes on within our modern research universities arises, not from departments, not from the university as a whole, not even from major professional associations, but from the vast network of subcommunities that form within and across university cultures. I have already commented upon this fact when I remarked that UCLA is less than the sum of its parts. Many of these study groups

or organizations that cut across established departmental lines do more
or less approximate what I have described as spirited communities of
learning. This may be the single most important and most ignored fact
about university life today.

Let me now consider third the group mentioned earlier, the Chicago
Group on the History of the Social Sciences, as an illustration of this
situation. Though it has changed its name to the Workshop in the History of the Human Sciences, it has continued to flourish, meeting regularly, much as it had in 1982 when I left, to discuss matters such as
professionalization and historical method. The four historians I knew
best in that group—Jan Goldstein, Robert Richards, Peter Novick, and
George Stocking—have since published major works that were shaped
very much by the conversations that took place during and after those
meetings.[5] In other words, the group was in 1982 and has remained one
of those subcommunities whose activities manifest the kind of spirited
inquiry I have outlined in Chapter 3. As I and others remember our
conversations back then, most of the participants really did offer their
criticisms of one another benevolently, and in thereby wishing one
another well, they displayed one of the essential elements of friendship.

My only way of keeping my friendship with Jan and George and Bob
and Peter alive has been through my reading of their books and occasionally responding to them. As I have already written to one or another
of them, I can discern in their writings the exercise of such virtues as
charity, humility, and justice, virtues that account in large measure for
the strength and the persuasive force of their historical analyses. Yet
they would not, so far as I know or remember, choose to characterize
their work primarily in these terms. Instead, they speak to one another
and to other members of the historical profession in terms of multicon-
textual explanation, overdetermination, and internalist as opposed to
externalist accounts of the history of the natural sciences or the social
sciences. Although this professional vocabulary reveals the common
methods and procedures that characterize all of their writings, it ob-
scures their deeper moral sources. I would submit that the motive that
impels each of them to adopt these methods is a tacit commitment to a
kind of substantive rationality that informs the purely procedural rationality that they and Weber before them emphasized, the desire to realize
in their writings a particular good—a just and true treatment of their
subject(s).

Readers like them who are participating in the conversation of this book will be persuaded less by its arguments and more by honest reflection upon their own past or present educational experience. The modern research university is so captivated by the Weberian ethos that many of its best citizens can no longer recognize either themselves or the deepest sources of their own learning. Thus, the ideal-typical model of the university outlined in the first chapter is more of a utopia (in the negative sense) than the spirited communities of learning described previously. Our goal should therefore be to recognize the truth about what activities and contexts most enable us to flourish as academics, a truth that is currently obscured by the notion that our own work just is publication and by the notion that our moral commitments are purely procedural. Once we recognize the truth of our condition, we then need to include our students fully within the experience of community that many of us have already to some extent found.

Question: Could not much of what you recommend here be readily accomplished by sharpening the distinction between the American college and the American university?

Consideration: It would be convenient if we had available to us in fact or in theory distinctions like the following:

> A University embodies the principle of progress, and a College that of stability; the one is the sail, and the other the ballast; each is insufficient in itself for the pursuit, extension, and inculcation of knowledge; each is useful to the other. A University is the scene of enthusiasm, of pleasurable exertion, of brilliant display, of winning influence, of diffusive and potent sympathy; and a College is the scene of order, of obedience, of modest and persevering diligence, of conscientious fulfillment of duty, of mutual private services, and deep and lasting attachments. . . . The University is for theology, law, and medicine, for natural history, for physical science . . . ; the College is for the formation of character, intellectual and moral, for the cultivation of the mind, for the improvement of the individual, for the study of literature, for the classics, and those rudimental sciences that strengthen and sharpen the intellect.[6]

Those of us who still feel the force of these sentiments and who recognize them as Newman's must realize also, with J. M. Cameron, that they belong to a vanished world.[7] The distinctions never did become clearly embodied in the arrangement of educational institutions in the United States, and though they still do obtain to some extent in England, they survive as remnants of an earlier educational establishment that has become since Newman's time quite thoroughly secularized.

To think that we could reintroduce distinctions like these into the present United States is at best to be afflicted with a severe case of terminal wistfulness. Very few colleges in this country have the self-assurance, the endowment strength, and the depth of spiritual conviction to resist the external constraints placed upon them by accrediting agencies, professional schools, and the modern research university. Strong, independent-minded four-year colleges that honor a tradition of education in and for thoughtfulness should be supported as wholeheartedly as possible, but too few exist to constitute by themselves a national strategy. The few church-related colleges and universities that still do take their religious affiliations seriously could be the nucleus of a potentially saving remnant, however.

Question: Does not this latter observation vindicate church-related higher education at the expense of the secular academy, an intention denied in the Preface?

Considerations: In order effectively to challenge the Weberian hegemony described in Chapter 1, we need multiple strategies. The informing principle behind all of them must be, as I have suggested, a reconception of the academic vocation that places teaching and learning at the heart and center of the academic enterprise. One such strategy was pursued with a considerable measure of success by the Danforth Foundation during the 1950s and 1960s. The genius of Danforth was precisely to construe the relationship between religion and higher learning as fundamentally a vocational problem facing prospective college and university teachers. The foundation sought, especially in its fellowship programs, to create genuine gatherings of friends who were and would remain bound together by a common commitment to education in and for thoughtfulness. According to the Danforth model of excellence, human beings could not fully think through important questions of human concern unless they were also considerate of the thoughts and lives of others. And they could not be fully thoughtful in this latter sense without being existentially serious about religious matters. The example of Danforth demonstrates that alternative, institutionalized models of academic excellence need not be either invidiously sectarian or terminally wistful.

Parker Palmer's writings evince the influence of his long period of
service to the work of the Danforth Foundation, and they suggest a
second strategy for countering the Weberian ethos. It is really a kind of
extension of the Danforth approach without the support networks that
Danforth provided or inspired. Palmer suggests that genuine change
within the academy will result only if individual teachers discipline
themselves first and then seek to display and encourage the practices of
the relevant spiritual virtues in classrooms everywhere. He does not call
for massive structural changes or significant curricular innovations in
American higher education. He instead stresses thoughtfulness about
commitment to pedagogy and community.

A third strategy does involve strengthening those church-related or
religiously affiliated institutions of higher learning that have maintained
a clear sense of their own distinctive vocations in the world of higher
learning. David Riesman and Christopher Jencks were correct when
they wrote the following, in 1968, about Roman Catholic higher education: "The important question . . . is not whether a few Catholic universities prove capable of competing with Harvard and Berkeley on the
latter's terms, but whether Catholicism can provide an ideology or personnel for developing alternatives to the Harvard-Berkeley model of
excellence."[8] We need very much to remember this insight as it applies
to all religiously affiliated colleges and universities, for it points to the
kind of pluralism that is most healthy for the world of higher learning, an
institutional pluralism that is based upon alternative models of human
excellence.

Question: Will not your "communities" of higher learning, especially the religious communities you have just mentioned, finally stultify
inquiry, which is often linked to disagreement and conflict rather than to
consensus and harmony?

Considerations: One of my former students who has since become a
colleague once complained about what he called a "cult of niceness"
that had grown up temporarily at the university where I currently teach.
He was describing by that strange phrase what I gather underlies the
present objection, the fear of and the opposition to intellectual oppres-
sion that takes the form of an overt pretense of community combined
with a covert persecution of those regarded as deviants. In the name of
community, public conflict is repressed; superficial charity becomes a

kiss of intellectual betrayal. The situation described here really would
stultify inquiry, which does depend, as the question assumes, upon open
and productive conflict.

But this situation is also the antithesis of community as I understand it
and as I have therefore attempted to characterize it. According to that
account, academic community, the place where human beings are drawn
together through the practice of such spiritual virtues as humility and
charity, enables, even promotes, productive conflict. Covert competi-
tion, not overt conflict, is the main enemy of this form of community.

Parker Palmer has made this point forcefully in speaking of community in the classroom:

> A healthy community, while it may exclude this one-up, one-down
> thing called competition, includes conflict at its very heart, checking
> and correcting and enlarging the knowledge of individuals by drawing
> on the knowledge of the group. Healthy conflict is possible only in the
> context of supportive community. What prevents conflicts in our
> classrooms is a simple emotion called fear. It is fear that is in the
> hearts of teachers as well as students. It is fear of exposure, of appear-
> ing ignorant, of being ridiculed. And the only antidote to that fear is a
> hospitable environment created, for example, by a teacher who knows
> how to use every remark, no matter how mistaken or seemingly stu-
> pid, to upbuild both the individual and the group. . . . Community
> is not opposed to conflict. On the contrary, community is precisely
> that place where an arena for creative conflict is protected by the
> compassionate fabric of human caring itself.[9]

Question: When you seek to illustrate the interdependence of intellectual and spiritual virtues, you rely exclusively upon examples from the
humanities—history, literature, philosophy. Can you seriously mean to
exclude the social and the natural sciences from your discussion?

Considerations: My exclusions here are an index of my ignorance.
Teaching, learning, and research in the social sciences have become, if
anything, more rather than less dependent upon the exercise of spiritual
virtues, ever since the emergence of what has been called the "interpretive turn" within disciplines like anthropology, political science, sociology, even economics. The natural sciences will probably prove especially instructive here, however, because the objectivist epistemology
arose originally from the ranks of physicists and mathematicians or from
philosophers who based their theorizing upon (sometimes dubious) ex-

trapolations from the work of these natural sciences. The extreme and therefore the most revealing test case would be the teaching and learning of advanced mathematics.

A growing body of information, some of it anecdotal, some of it based upon extensive research, suggests that the same things we have been saying about the teaching and learning of history apply to the teaching and learning of mathematics. Spiritual and intellectual virtues are interdependent. Students learn mathematics better the more the process of learning involves the cultivation of spiritual virtues. Models of learning that are based upon highly individualistic and competitive understandings of mathematical education are, by any standards of measurement, deficient.

One of the most impressive studies that support these claims is the evaluation of the Mathematics Workshop Program (MWP) of the University of California at Berkeley. Concerned faculty members had been puzzled and alarmed by the low achievements of African American undergraduates in comparison to their Asian American counterparts in beginning calculus courses. After an extensive ethnographic study of the study habits and social patterns of these two groups, researchers discovered that Chinese students were much more inclined to organize themselves into study groups than were African American students. Moreover, the social dimension of learning among Chinese students was "a critical component of each student's mastery of calculus."[10]

On the basis of this finding, the MWP arranged workshops that contained a high percentage of African American and Hispanic students (80 percent). These workshops were conducted very much like the informal study groups that Asian American students had arranged for themselves. ". . . Students help each other to solve . . . problems and to understand the ideas on which the problems are based; however, there are no fixed rules regarding how students must proceed." All students must be willing "at some point during the workshop session to share their ideas and to critique the work of their peers."[11]

The results of these workshops were even more dramatic than their creators had expected. For example, from 1978 to 1982, 54 percent of African American students who participated in the MWP earned a grade of B-minus or better in the introductory calculus course. By contrast, only 16 percent of those African American students who did not participate in the MWP earned a grade of B-minus or better during the same period of time. These dramatic differences appear consistently between

MWP and non-MWP students within subgroups defined by sex, Economic Opportunity Program status, SAT-Math triads, or engineer/ nonengineer programs of study. In brief, the more the social dimension of learning was strengthened, the higher the level of individual achievement among all students.[12]

The experience of the MWP provides compelling evidence for the claim that the practice of virtues like benevolence, charity, and humility is integrally connected to the learning and teaching of mathematics, that we ignore the social dimension of intellect only at our own collective peril. But for our purposes here, we must bear in mind that the converse of this claim is also true. The manner of teaching calculus in this case also involved the cultivation of moral and spiritual virtues. To *require* that students be willing to help one another is the first step toward the formation of habits that together make spirited inquiry possible. In the case of the Berkeley students, these MWP practices did seem to become habitual for many. Their graduation rates were also appreciably higher than those of non-MWP students.

In sum, in whatever domain of higher learning we might examine, pedagogy has an ethical dimension. The question is not, Does the teaching of mathematics or physics or history *have* an ethical dimension? The only question for our purposes is, *Which* ethos does any given pedagogy promote?

Question: Are there ''spiritual virtues'' other than the five discussed here—faith, humility, self-denial, charity, and friendship—that are indispensable to learning?

Considerations: The moral and spiritual virtues that are indispensable to learning are many and various, so the five mentioned are by no means an exhaustive list. For our purposes here, two features of *most* of the virtues that might appear on any such list are crucial: first, they will tend to be social, impinging directly upon the quality of our relationships with others; second, they will tend to sustain community because of their historically religious character. We can, with these features in mind, extend the list by way of illustration, but there is no point in attempting to be exhaustive.

Consider, for examples, virtues like loyalty and hospitality. Under the redescription of the academic vocation offered here, we would come to place a higher premium upon loyalty to particular academic communities than we do currently. The amount of mobility that characterizes

life at the large research universities is more consistent with academics
as a career than it is with academics as a vocation. The virtue of hospitality involves the whole crucially important matter of how we treat
those who are strangers to our way of thinking and being. The cultivation and exercise of this virtue, more than any other, protect communities against both tribalism and bland uniformity in thought and action.
More extended and precise descriptions of these and other virtues that
are deeply implicated in the activities of teaching and learning are subjects for another book.

Question: Most eighteen-year-olds are already fully formed (or deformed, as the case may be) when they arrive at colleges and universities. Might it not be therefore very difficult, if not impossible, to form
students' characters once they reach the university?

Considerations: Of all the questions thus far raised, this is the most
troubling. The questions of the extent to which and the manner in which
colleges and universities can actually shape students' characters have
been matters of extensive study in the behavioral sciences over the
course of the last thirty years. We will therefore examine some of that
literature in the next chapter. Recently, however, largely as a result of
the influence of Allan Bloom's *The Closing of the American Mind,* many
academics have come to think that the characters of today's students are
so deformed that it is pointless for the academy to seek to instill new
habits in the vast majority of them. This is an ironic development,
because Bloom ostensibly sought to demonstrate how the university had
"impoverished the souls of today's students," not how the students had
impoverished the aspirations of the university.

Nevertheless, Bloom's fulminations against young people have in
large part accounted for the phenomenal popularity of his book. And if
Bloom is correct, it *would* be misguided to attempt to shape students'
characters in college. In his judgment, the souls of today's students are
so shrunken and deformed that it is inconceivable that anyone or
anything, least of all the university by any description, could further
impoverish them, or begin to restore them to health for that matter. The
first third of *The Closing of the American Mind,* entitled "Students,"
characterizes today's young people as virtually uneducable. Because
they have not been nourished on great books, they enter college without
"that refinement of the mind's eye that permits it to see the delicate
distinctions among men, among their deeds and their motives."[13] Mu-

sic, but only rock music, is *"the* youth culture," all rock music reduces
to Mick Jaggerism, and Mick Jaggerism creates the typical thirteen-
year-old "whose body throbs with orgasmic rhythms; whose feelings
are made articulate in hymns to the joys of onanism or the killing of
parents; whose ambition is to win fame and wealth in imitating the drag-
queen who makes the music. In short, life is made into a nonstop,
commercially prepackaged masturbational fantasy."[14]

What are those of us who do think that a proper college education
might make young people more thoughtful human beings to do with
such cranky but widely accepted characterizations of "today's students"? We might try to extract from Bloom's text what is well considered and well tempered. So, for example, we might wonder with him
about "whether the experience of the greatest texts from early childhood
is not a prerequisite for a concern throughout life for them and for lesser
but important literature."[15] The answer to this question is by no means
certain, but the question is worth considering anew, with instruction
from *some* of Bloom's discussion and from other sources that impinge in
various ways upon it, such as E. D. Hirsch's *Cultural Literacy* and
Northrop Frye's *The Educated Imagination.*

Or we might pursue another and more fruitful line of inquiry in view
of Bloom's characterization (really caricature) of "today's students."
Suppose that Bloom is right: suppose today's students really are unable
to recognize, much less appreciate, excellence; deafened by orgiastic
music; and incapable of love. Why try to teach them? Aristotle, in the
Nicomachean Ethics, was firm and clear about this matter. The teaching
of political science, which was, for him, *the* architectonic science that
investigated all of the questions that Bloom quite properly believes to be
at the center of academic life, was, Aristotle believed, utterly wasted on
the young. For, "since the young man tends to follow his passions, his
study will be vain and unprofitable. . . . And it makes no difference
whether he is young in years or youthful in character; the defect does not
depend on time, but on his living, and pursuing each successive object,
as passion directs."[16]

The danger in Bloom's diatribe against today's students stems from
the passion behind it, a passion that in turn panders to a mood that, from
time to time, overtakes all of us who care about higher education. The
virtue of Aristotle's restrained and direct statement of the issue is that it
forces us to examine ourselves, to see how seriously we really take our
own occasionally despairing judgments about the young, and to consider

the implications of those judgments for the ways in which we have chosen to live and learn and teach. Which college teacher has not voiced sentiments very similar to Bloom's about several students' lack of wonder about the world, their apparent indifference in the presence of high and excellent things, their sordid and confused longings, and their strange tastes for noise as opposed to music? Bloom takes these commonplace observations and ordinary frustrations, dresses them up in portentous phrases, and offers them to us as definitive cultural pronouncements. Aristotle, with great verbal economy and with no interest in merely inflaming our irritations, forces us to wonder about what should be taught to whom at what time. Aristotle provokes questioning; Bloom, in his discussion of today's students, merely provokes.

The most urgent and controversial question provoked by both Aristotle and the question presently before us is really this: Is academic life as it is here redescribed really appropriate for everyone over eighteen? The answer must clearly be no. Some people, young and old alike, simply refuse to see the *facts* of the matter, namely that certain actions and ways of life are noble and certain others are ignoble. These persons lack "moral education" altogether—they are suffering, as Martha Nussbaum notes, from *apaideusia,* the disease of the Cyclopes—and they are therefore not fit candidates for the academy, which is not a place for those who are at best *beginning* a process of spiritual and intellectual development.[17]

Students in other words *must* be properly formed *to some extent* before they can begin to strengthen the practice of those spiritual and intellectual virtues that will constitute a life of human flourishing for them and others. They must want to do better at the right sorts of things and so seek to improve themselves in and by doing them. These practices will in turn have cognitive implications, for they will be the main way that students learn what is truly noble. Likewise, when they come to *reflect* upon their actions and practices—what should be the main business of the academic study of ethics—their thinking will lead to more virtuous behavior. Thus, the following description of Aristotle's *Nicomachean Ethics* applies to much of academic life as I have sought here to redescribe it:

> [Aristotle] is giving a course in practical thinking to enable someone who already wants to be virtuous to understand better what he should do and why. Such understanding, as Aristotle conceives it, is more than merely cognitive. Since it is the articulation of a mature scheme

of values under the heading of the good, it will itself provide new and more reflective motivation for virtuous conduct. That is why Aristotle can claim that the goal of the study of ethics is action, not merely knowledge: to become fully virtuous rather than simply to know what virtue requires. Someone with a sense of shame will respond, because he wants to do better at the right sorts of things. Someone with nothing but fear of punishment will not respond; the only thing to do with him is tell him what he will get into trouble for.''[18]

In sum, the present question arises from a proper concern about extreme instances, but it is mistaken about a substantial majority of students. The souls of most college students are formed to a great extent, but they are by no means fully formed. Those students who are un-formed (*apaideusia*) and those who are wholly deformed should not be admitted to the academy. In order to be admitted to a course of academic study, students must be to some extent *well* formed already. Otherwise, as Aristotle has said, their education will be wasted.

Question: The shape and purposes of higher learning are not only limited by the capacity and the will of other institutions, such as fami-lies, schools, and churches, to nurture the souls of young people. They are also limited and strongly conditioned by the ethos of the socio-economic system. Is not the ethos of contemporary culture in the United States fundamentally at odds with the ethos you are promoting here?

Considerations: We should be wary of such sweeping claims, but we ought also to acknowledge that the Weberian ethos described in Chapter 1 does have many affinities with both the expressive individualism and the utilitarian individualism that Bellah and his colleagues found so widely prevalent in American society. Thus, if the understanding of academic vocation as I have here outlined it *were* widely adopted in practice, the university would become to some extent countercultural. It would emphasize learning and teaching for the sake of serving and edifying others, not primarily for the sake of self-fulfillment, self-aggrandizement, and mastery of the world. Understanding and service would supersede manipulation and control.

These stark contrasts are not very helpful, however, because, as Charles Taylor has shown, modern morality has many sources, and some of the best are still nurtured and sustained within the secular academy. More helpful perhaps is to recognize some of the socio-economic *consequences* of the academy's great emphasis upon technical training and procedural rationality. This recognition may help us to consider the concrete implications of a more countercultural understanding of the academic vocation.

In his book *The Work of Nations,* Robert Reich has demonstrated the preeminence of the United States in its capacity to train the most influential segment of the international labor force, symbolic analysts. These people "solve, identify, and broker problems by manipulating symbols." Symbolic analysts embrace an enormous array of occupations; they are design engineers, software engineers, public relations executives, lawyers, creative accountants, real estate developers, organizational development specialists, editors, writers, consultants of all sorts, advertising executives, film editors, musicians, and marketing strategists.[19] Reich's description of their activities and their ethos involves a wedding of technologism (manipulation of symbols to solve problems) to expressive individualism (a making of knowledge as a form of self-expression). All university professors and a substantial proportion of university graduates fall under this description. We can, I think, agree with Reich and numerous university presidents that America's universities are far ahead of all foreign competitors in the education of symbolic analysts.

Having described the training and the character of symbolic analysts, Reich proceeds to present a rather frightful scenario: these people are virtually seceding (Reich's word) from their respective locales, even from their respective countries. Tied by modem and fax machines into a global web, symbolic analysts segregate themselves into research centers with their own security forces, their own health spas, their own private medical clinics, their own condominium complexes, in brief their own life-style enclaves.[20] American symbolic analysts are therefore much more loyal (if loyalty applies here at all) to their counterparts in Europe and Asia than they are to their poverty-stricken fellow citizens a few miles away. In sum, Reich gives us a brief and compelling portrait of the global, socioeconomic expression of purely technical rationality: life-style enclaves of specialists without spirit.

He is somewhat at a loss about what we can do about this alarming state of affairs beyond enforcing public policies such as truly progressive income taxes that would impel the very rich to share their wealth with the very poor. And by his own accounting, the modern research university is part of the "problem" rather than part of the solution. Our proposals here would involve, not so much a series of reforms as a reorientation in our thinking about teaching and learning. Thus, it is no surprise that symbolic analysts have little sense of public service or the common good if the universities are organized to give them purely technical skills of analysis, interpretation, and criticism with little or no attention in theory or practice to substantive moral goods. From such a point of view, it makes sense to send students abroad to study with their counterparts in Europe and Asia in a manner similar to the style they pursue here. If the aim of education is thoughtfulness, however, global education programs would look more like those at Goshen College, where students spend their time abroad living, studying, and serving in the homes of the poor, than like those at most other universities, where students study in enclaves of American students abroad or in universities that resemble our own. The kind of human being one becomes is very much dependent upon the kind of company one keeps, especially during the course of one's education.

We should admit, however, that Reich's overall argument raises some very disturbing implications for our own analysis thus far. For according to Reich, the education of symbolic analysts, unlike that of many other students, proceeds in many ways like the education we have recommended heretofore:

> Yet in America's best classrooms, again, the emphasis has shifted. Instead of individual achievement and competition, the focus is on group learning. Students learn to articulate, clarify, and then restate for one another how they identify and find answers. They learn how to seek and accept criticism from peers, solicit help, and give credit to others. They also learn to negotiate—to explain their own needs, to discern what others need and view things from others' perspectives, and to discover mutually beneficial resolutions. This is an ideal preparation for lifetimes of symbolic-analytical teamwork.[21]

Statements like these should make us realize that education in and for thoughtfulness needs to include *both* collaborative problem solving of the kind described here by Reich and manifested by the MWP at Berkeley *and* ethical inquiry into those goods most worth pursuing in human life. Collaborative learning does not by itself cultivate benevolence and altruism. In addition, certain particular questions must be kept alive by the university, *questions* such as, Who is your neighbor? Reich's book should make us wonder whether we have perhaps thus far stressed the manner of inquiry without giving appropriate correlative stress to the matter of it.

And Reich's findings should also remind us of our earlier worry over whether or not the weakening of the great religious traditions that emphasize concern for the hungry and the impoverished might result in the long run in an attenuation of those virtues that direct our energies toward serving the most marginalized among our brothers and sisters. As St. Augustine pointed out long ago, many of the virtues are honored and practiced even among thieves.

Question: This latter observation leads directly to the final question here. Does not the argument about the virtues that are necessary in order fully to pursue the truth of matters depend for its validity upon certain ontological claims? Does not the robust sense of piety defended in the preceding chapter make no sense if God does not exist?

Considerations: Piety in fact precedes, both logically and chronologically, the formulation of ontological claims of one sort or another. We must remember, however, that both the nontheistic piety of a Jeffrey Stout and the theistic piety of a James Gustafson suffice for the purpose of invigorating the spiritual virtues discussed here. Still, a certain ontological thesis is minimally required and therefore implied by much of what has been argued thus far. The thesis holds that there really is a way things are that is distinct from any and all of our versions of it, but that we are forever barred for all sorts of reasons from grasping the way things are completely. Let us call this the "through the glass darkly" thesis, because it is equally committed to the view that objects of all sorts truly exist apart from our descriptions and to the view that we cannot have unmediated access to them.

This thesis is sharply distinct from the view that there are *only* our invented versions of reality, and that we can therefore be said to make worlds at will. Indeed, some such understanding informs the defective *ethos* of the symbolic analysts we have just now mentioned. Their collective indifference to the lot of their less fortunate neighbors can perhaps be connected to their tacit conviction that the world is infinitely manipulable. We must turn now to the interconnections between this latter and pernicious ontology and the formation of the modern educated personality.

Notes

1. J. M. Cameron, *On the Idea of a University* (University of Toronto Press: Toronto, Buffalo, and London, 1978), 32.

2. James Turner and Paul Bernard, "The Prussian Road to the University? German Models and the University of Michigan, 1837–c. 1895," *Rackham Reports* (University of Michigan, 1988–89), 16.

3. *Hastings Center Report* 20 (January/February, 1990), 5.

4. Robert N. Bellah, Richard Madsen, William Sullivan, Ann Swidler, and Stephen M. Tipton, *Habits of the Heart: Individualism and Commitment in American Life* (Harper and Row: New York, 1986), 303.

5. Jan Goldstein, *Console and Classify: The French Psychiatric Profession in the Nineteenth Century* (Cambridge University Press: New York, 1989); Peter Novick, *That Noble Dream: The "Objectivity Question" and the American Historical Profession* (Cambridge University Press: New York, 1989); Robert J. Richards, *Darwin and the Emergence of Evolutionary Theories of Mind and Behavior* (University of Chicago Press: Chicago, 1987); George W. Stocking, Jr., *Victorian Anthropology* (Free Press: New York, 1987).

6. John Henry Cardinal Newman, *University Sketches* (The Walter Scott Publishing Company: London and New York, 1902), 222.

7. Cameron, *op. cit.*, 43.

8. *The Academic Revolution* (Doubleday and Company: Garden City, 1968), 405.

9. Parker Palmer, "Community, Conflict, and Ways of Knowing," *Change* (September/October, 1987), 25.

10. Robert E. Fullilove and Philip Uri Treisman, "Mathematics Achievement among African American Undergraduates at the University of California, Berkeley: An Evaluation of the Mathematics Workshop Program," *Journal of Negro Education* 59, 3 (1990), 465–66.

11. *Ibid.*, 468–69.

12. *Ibid.*, 474.

13. Allan Bloom, *The Closing of the American Mind* (Simon and Schuster: New York, 1987), 61.

14. *Ibid.*, 75.

15. *Ibid.*, 62.

16. Aristotle, *The Nicomachean Ethics*, trans. W. D. Ross (Oxford University Press: New York, 1986), book 1, part 3, 3–4.

17. Martha Nussbaum, *The Fragility of Goodness: Luck and Ethics in Greek Tragedy and Philosophy* (Cambridge University Press: New York, 1988), 252: "Now *apaedeusia* is not stupidity, absurdity, logical error, even wrongheadedness. It is lack of *paedeia,* the education by practice and precept that initiates a

young Greek into the ways of his community; the word is usually translated 'acculturation' or 'moral education.'"

18. M. F. Burnyeat, "Aristotle on Learning to Be Good," in Amelie Rorty, ed., *Essays on Aristotle's Ethics* (University of California Press: Los Angeles, 1980), 81.

19. Robert B. Reich, *The Work of Nations* (Alfred A. Knopf: New York, 1991), 177–78.

20. *Ibid.*, 268–71.

21. *Ibid.*, 233.

5

Adams's Education

I

The argument of this book has been based upon one major assumption, namely that epistemologies have ethical implications, that ways of knowing are not morally neutral but morally directive. Accordingly, the major contrast developed thus far has been between the Weberian epistemology that connects knowledge fundamentally to power, to the prospect of technical mastery of the world, and communitarian epistemologies that connect knowledge fundamentally to understanding, to the pursuit of the truth of matters. This broadly articulated contrast has in turn informed two distinct conceptions of academic life and of the nature and purpose of the academic vocation. On one account, the soul of the university is *Wissenschaft,* on the other, edification.

My discussion, in this epistemological and ethical context, of religious matters, especially the suggestion that certain spiritual virtues are indispensable to learning, has thus far been justified primarily on historical grounds. I have tried to show, first, that the Weberian conception of the academic calling derived in part from a transmutation of religious terms, and second, that for most of Western history religion and higher learning were interdependent in ways that have largely escaped the notice of many present-day analysts of the university. Then, in Chapter 3, I tried to demonstrate that, in spite of the triumph of Weberianism, practices that are central to the academy, such as teaching, learning, and scholarship, still depend for their success upon the exercise of spiritual virtues like charity.

If these observations are correct, my analysis and criticism of the current understanding of the academic vocation are not yet complete. For the following questions arise: Why do so many contemporary academics believe that their sense of vocation ought to conform to the ideal type developed by Weber even as they at the same time resonate to the more spiritualized conception of teaching and learning articulated by Parker Palmer? Is there a peculiarly modern and secular spirituality that gives a deep measure of meaning to the academic vocation as Weber described it and at the same time blinds its practitioners to their own necessary reliance upon virtues that are distinctively religious? Finally, if there is such a distinctively modernist account of our spiritual condition that informs current conceptions of higher learning, does it really improve upon earlier, religious accounts of our spiritual condition?

I wish now to complete my analysis and critique of the academic vocation by attending to these questions. In order to do so effectively, I will need to enlarge the meaning of the term *spiritual* beyond its strictly historical sense. I have thus far used the term to designate those virtues that arose within religious communities. I will now be using it in a broader sense, similar to the one used by Charles Taylor in his book *Sources of the Self,* to refer to that which finally gives our lives meaningful shape and purpose. I will therefore seek to complete my inquiry into the nature of the academic vocation by connecting the problem of modern education to the larger problem of the quest for meaning in our culture.

In order to do this in a focused and therefore manageable way, I want to turn to a sustained study of a twentieth-century literary work that, more than any other modernist classic, makes this connection between education and the modern quest for meaning explicit, *The Education of Henry Adams.* Perhaps the best way to expose the spiritual dimensions of the problem of the academic calling is through an examination of the lives and works of individuals like Henry Adams who actually suffered through, worried over, and finally helped to create the very situation that we now seek to comprehend. It may seem a peculiar undertaking to evoke spiritual ideas from a classic of modernism, but, as I shall try to show here, architects of modernity like Adams, James Joyce, and Marcel Proust construed their projects in spiritual terms. Thus, to speak of them and their undertakings in these terms is not to impose upon them an

alien vocabulary; it is rather to apprehend them and the meaning of the
intellectual world they helped to shape in the categories that they applied
to themselves.

There are three additional reasons for concluding this study by close
and critical attention to *The Education of Henry Adams.* First, as I will
show in the next section, Adams's *Education* is the most elaborate
portrayal, a fully realized prototype, of what many educators have subsequently offered as a description of the cognitive and ethical development of twentieth-century college students and faculty. Second, Adams
makes clear to us the many sources of what is perhaps the most
widespread and uncritically held assumption about spiritual formation in
our times: namely, that our lives have meaning *only* insofar as we create
that meaning *for ourselves* through language and other forms of expression. Third, by attending in the last part of this chapter to the relationship between Adams's life and his *Education,* we will be able briefly to
review and synthesize some of the most important aspects of our entire
study by observing how Henry Adams actually lived through them,
imbuing them as he did so with some of the articulate vitality that they
have retained to the present day.

Once we have understood Adams's story of education as the prototype of our own culture's story, we will then in the concluding chapter
appraise its strengths and limitations by contrasting it to the earlier and
more explicitly religious stories that Adams, like Weber, had subverted
in the course of "creating" modernity. Because I think that education
must finally involve the pursuit of the truth of matters, I will try in the
conclusion to assess the truth of Adams's *Education* relative to the truth
of Adam's education in the book of Genesis.

II

Hannah Arendt isolated, in *The Human Condition,* what is arguably the
most important signal element in that congeries of intellectual impulses
that has come to be known as modernism. She analyzed what she called
the ascendancy of *homo faber* over *homo sapiens,* the triumph of the
human being understood as the one who makes or creates over the
human being understood as the one who seeks or possesses wisdom.[1]
We have here been to some extent confirming Arendt's analysis in the
course of our critical examination of the most characteristic and perhaps

the most powerful institution of modernity, the research university. We have shown that *Wissenschaft,* or *making* knowledge, is the soul of that enterprise. We shall now extend Arendt's analysis in two ways. First, we shall elaborate one of the most important recent accounts of cognitive and ethical development among college students, noting its emphasis upon the human being as a fabricating animal. Second, we shall expose the spiritual and cultural roots of that account, as well as a powerful critique of it, in *The Education of Henry Adams.*

The twentieth-century ascendancy of *homo faber* can be discerned in the very title of William G. Perry, Jr.'s, widely read and still very much discussed 1981 account of student development during the college years, "Cognitive and Ethical Growth: The *Making* of Meaning."[2] Perry and a team of more than thirty associates had done much of the work that led to this formulation over a period of fifteen years at Harvard University during the 1950s and 1960s. The theory developed on the basis of that work was published in 1970 as *Forms of Intellectual and Ethical Development in the College Years.*[3] Since that time, Perry's work has spawned countless research projects designed to test, challenge, and modify what quickly became known as the "Perry scheme" of cognitive and ethical growth. Probably most of those educators who have sought to study the scheme directly have encountered it in its 1981 elaboration, which includes thoughtful responses to scores of critics and sympathizers, some of whom had been inspired to study cognitive and ethical development in part by the example of Perry and his Harvard associates.

According to Perry, college students may proceed through as many as nine positions or "stages of development" in the course of their intellectual life. Each stage represents a cognitive structure, a set of assumptions that determine how a given student will perceive, organize, and evaluate experience. The nine stages are invariably sequential in that students proceed through them one at a time in the same order. They are, moreover, qualitatively different from one another in that the passage from one stage to the next does *not* mean "adding more of the same" but rather thinking in a new way. Finally, the stages are hierarchical in that each stage incorporates the previous stage's rationale before broadening and transforming its assumptions.

The overwhelming majority of students at all colleges fall, according to Perry, somewhere between stages I and III. They are located in what he calls the "dualistic" phase. Dualists believe that there are two and only two categories: right and wrong. They moreover believe in what the philosopher Karl Popper once called the "empty bucket" theory of knowledge. Such students are self-styled empty vessels ready to be filled with truth, *that is,* right answers. Stages I, II, and III differ only according to how dualists account for uncertainty. In stage I, they refuse to recognize it: all information is either right or wrong. In stage II, they believe that apparent uncertainty is really the result of an error committed by a "wrong" authority. In stage III, dualists come to think that some uncertainty is genuine, but they believe that it is merely the temporary result of a localized lack of scholarly progress.[4]

Dualists predictably have great difficulty with certain academic tasks. They can seldom, if ever, acknowledge the legitimacy of conflicting points of view. They believe that classroom discussion is always a "waste of time." They prefer lectures, "objective" tests, and writing assignments that ask a question to which there can be only one "right" answer. They love tightly structured classroom situations.

Students in stages IV through VI despise tight structures. They are the multiplists. For them, all opinions do matter, and each opinion is or might be as good as the teacher's. They therefore often subscribe to the "one-sophomore-one-vote" theory of literary or historical or philosophical interpretation. No lectures for them: lecturing seems a form of tyranny. Truth occupies a small portion of the larger realm of knowledge, which is characterized by uncertainty. By stage VI, the multiplists have become relativists who claim that right-wrong dualism is legitimate for some types of inquiry but insist that all truths are finally conditional. Multiplists thrive on assignments that dualists cannot comprehend. They like to enumerate several conflicting opinions or interpretations and adjudicate among them.[5]

The need to adopt a reasoned point of view that is coherent, consistent, and logically defensible leads some students from multiplicity into committed contextual relativism (stages VII through IX). Perry admits that these last three stages represent positions of psychosocial rather than purely cognitive development. Students in stages IV through VI often feel lost in a world of uncertainty (all of Perry's stages have affective as well as cognitive dimensions), and most multiplists seem to remain uncertain, cynical, and uncommitted for their entire college career. Some multiplists, however, "graduate" into commitment, recognizing the need to assume reasoned responsibility for their life choices.

Others unfortunately retreat into dualism with an antiintellectual vengeance.[6]

Perry has applied this scheme with a considerable amount of sensitivity and dexterity. He has noted, for example, that the scheme is recursive.[7] When any one of us seeks to enter a new field of learning, we typically begin as dualists. "Which books should we read?" we often ask authorities whom we trust. We then move through a phase when we are overwhelmed with what seem to be competing but equally plausible points of view. And we finally emerge with a set of convictions about which one of the several viewpoints seems most rationally compelling. Though the Perry scheme was designed to explain *student* behavior, it applies just as much to teachers. Indeed, many faculty, having been educated in the same system that they serve, remain forever in stages IV through VI as multiplists without inner direction or settled convictions. University professors have become very proficient at freeing students *from* the tyranny of those unexamined prejudices that hold sway over their minds, even though many of these professors have no belief about what they are freeing the students *for*.

Long before Perry and his co-workers discerned recurrent patterns of cognitive development at Harvard, Henry Adams, himself a Harvard graduate and later a Harvard professor, had begun to experience life as a "double thing." His *Education* begins with a series of unforgettable dualisms—Boston and Quincy, winter and summer, discipline and freedom, error and truth. In the course of his quest for some master generalization that would "finish his clamor to be educated," Adams repeatedly failed, until he adopted a position that he himself called "multiplicity." Finally, Adams devised a "formula of his own," arguing, again as Perry later would, that meaning is something that we make, not something that we find.

Unlike Perry, however, Adams realized that he was very much, perhaps too much, a creature of his own time and place. He came of age during the nineteenth century when developmental models were everywhere in fashion. Yet he derided the safe and self-congratulatory overtones of Comtean and Darwinian conceptions of "progress" regardless of whether such conceptions were applied to the human mind, as they were, during Adams's lifetime, by Herbert Spencer, or to nations and cultures, as they were by E. B. Tylor. Adams accordingly arranged his *Education* to challenge the prevailing smug faith in developmentalisms of all sorts. He seldom missed an opportunity to insist that his world was devolving more than it was evolving. And he interpreted his life not as a smooth, linear progression through stages but rather as a series of convulsive discontinuities.

Adams's *Education* thus displayed movement and change but not some idealized and ahistorical model of progress. He had modeled his *Education* in part on the great spiritual autobiography of St. Augustine. And he was careful and astute enough to observe that whereas Augustine in the *Confessions* had worked from multiplicity to unity, he had been *forced* to reverse this movement and to work from unity to multiplicity. He moreover stated precisely, in terms that were very similar to Weber's, those conditions of the modern West that made his journey through life so different from Augustine's: technological change, the increased velocity of history, the rise of modern science, centralization and concentration of political power, and the "stupendous failure of Christianity."

Though we may disagree with Adams about the formative conditions of our world, we should imitate him in one respect when we reflect upon the significance of the work of Perry, his followers, and his critics. We should first strive to see Perry's research as the *kind* of work it really is, and we should then bring to bear upon it the same kind of cultural and historical perspective that Adams applied to his own education. Seen from such a vantage point, Perry's work looks like the modern, secular equivalent of a medieval manual of spiritual discipline. It stands in relation to Adams's *Education* in much the same way that the manuals of religious orders once stood in relation to a single, great spiritual autobiography.

On this interpretation, the Perry scheme really marks out the nine stages of the soul's movement from ignorance to enlightenment or from innocence to maturity. It also informs the modern, secular priesthood of college and university professors about those pedagogical disciplines best designed to accelerate such a movement, and it promises that, if followed "religiously," the program will lead devotees to the saving graces of committed contextual relativism. According to this reading, the Perry scheme tells us very little about the growth of the *human mind* (whatever that term might mean apart from culture and community). Instead, it tells us a great deal about the process of acculturation we have devised in the United States over the course of the last century. After his colleagues had shown him the powerful prescriptive element in his account of student development, Perry argued quite openly that teaching and the curriculum should be "optimally designed to invite, encourage, challenge, and support students in such development. Our scheme, therefore, is helpful to the extent that it contributes to the ability of planners and teachers to *communicate* with students who make meaning in different ways and to provide differential opportunities for their progress."[8]

Some devotees of Perry have come mistakenly to think that *all* minds either must or should (the distinction is seldom made clearly) develop in the same way that Adams's did. Whereas Adams always insisted his *Education* was more about his times than about his life, many present-day educators accept the Perry scheme as an immutable and universal law of human cognitive development. Adams, the prototypical multiplist, knew full well that his own journey from unity to multiplicity was an aberration in the context of the larger movement of Western history. Even so, many people today unfortunately view the same journey as a law of nature rather than an artifact of culture.

Adams's *Education* thus reveals the limitations of the Perry scheme even as it serves as an inspiration for it. Once these limitations are fully appreciated, college and university teachers can learn a great deal from Perry. The movement that Perry describes and documents is, after all, a *fact* of contemporary cultural life. Once that movement is properly understood, teachers can better interpret the contradictory and therefore puzzling course evaluations they receive. They can also learn why many students have great difficulty understanding, much less completing, their assignments. And, as Perry has said, faculty can "save wasted effort and maximize the effort expended" by securing "a better understanding of where different students are 'coming from.' "[9]

Academics should also be troubled, however, by some of the more fundamental questions that Perry's work raises. According to Perry and his imposingly large number of sympathetic researchers, American colleges and universities today send forth into the world an enormous number of cynical and disaffected multiplists. Are these students the casualties of poor teaching or are they, as the present study suggests they might be, the kind of graduates one should expect from the modern research university? Are our methods faulty, or are our present educational aspirations questionable? Should we continue uncritically to pursue making meaning and making knowledge as the constitutive activities of higher learning? Or is the goal of edification in and for thoughtfulness more worthy of our collective ambitions?

In order properly to address these questions, we must examine more closely the assumption that finally unites Perry, Adams, and Weber. Is *homo faber* the last and only word about humankind, or is there still something to be said for *homo sapiens?* Granted the obvious truth that we all to some extent make meaning in and of our lives, are there limits to our fabrications? Or can we completely make our world and ourselves? We shall turn now to these theological matters through a more extensive consideration of Adams's *Education.*

III

By studying *The Education of Henry Adams* and then examining the relevant aspects of the life of its author, we will gain access to the inner workings of the emergence of modernity. The modern research university is an integral part of that larger historical process, as we have seen. What we will now discover through our study of Adams is that modernity is itself based upon a set of transformations not unlike the ones we examined in our study of Weber's notions of the academy and the academic vocation. Weber subverted a religious tradition. Adams and other modernists subverted a religious myth of creation. Much of modern education has therefore come to be a kind of aspiration to deity, a willful move to ignore and perhaps to violate the lessons of Eden. Thus, the problem of modern education is to some extent a theological problem. We shall come to see this more clearly through an examination first of Adams's *Education* and then of his life.

The Education of Henry Adams is in every way a manifestation of modernity. Its form and meaning are so elusive that critics of the work have not been able to agree even upon what *genre* of writing it exemplifies. At one time or another, the work has been reckoned a history, an autobiography, a piece of realist fiction, or an extended prose poem. Adams's contemporaries tried to understand the *Education* in terms of realistic historical narration, and they judged it according to the accuracy of its detail and the plausibility of its interpretation.[10] More recent critics have emphasized its elaborate artifice.[11] Refusing to consider it a conventional transcription of Adams's past, they have maintained that

Adams manipulated, even deliberately distorted, historical figures and events for the sake of exclusively literary purposes. They have accordingly mooted questions of historical accuracy and have focused instead upon questions of rhetorical form—upon the language, the symbolic structure, and the tone of the work. Whatever the final verdict, both the character and the range of critical disagreement attest to the *Education*'s modernity. One of the distinctive characteristics of modernism has been the conflation, sometimes the violation, of established generic categories.

Although the *Education* is difficult to categorize, its essential purposes can be grasped most firmly by placing it in the company of contemporary masterpieces by James Joyce and Marcel Proust. In 1904, one year before Adams finished the *Education,* the young Joyce began to write what ultimately became, after some ten years of revision, *A Portrait of the Artist as a Young Man.* A few years later, Proust gathered his extensive notes together, retreated into his cork-lined apartment, and began work on his monumental *Remembrance of Things Past.* Like the two much younger writers, Adams found it necessary to develop a new literary formula in order to present his sense of the world, and, like them, he settled upon one that was quasi-autobiographical in nature.

This convergence of Adams, Joyce, and Proust illustrates what one critic has called the inherent tendency of realist fiction toward autobiography.[12] Speaking of the intellectual background of *A Portrait of the Artist,* this same critic made a general observation about the modern writer that applies exactly to Henry Adams.

> The forces which make him an outsider focus his observation upon himself. He becomes his own hero, and begins to crowd other characters into the background. The background takes on a new importance for its influence upon his own character. The theme of this novel is the formation of character; its habitual pattern is that of apprenticeship and education.[13]

In the same year in which he mailed to several friends a privately printed copy of his *Education,* Adams wrote to one of them an appraisal of the book that confirms this latter-day critical judgment in terms of Adams's explicitly stated intentions.

> An experiment like this volume [the *Education*] is hazardous, not as history, but as art. To write a heavy dissertation on modern education, and fill up the background with moving figures that will carry the load,

is a literary *tour-de-force* that cannot wholly succeed even in the hands of St. Augustine or Rousseau.[14]

In brief, Adams closed his career precisely where Joyce and Proust began, composing a work that described the development of the very sensibility that in turn made the work about that development possible. Thus, in terms of both its form and its subject matter, the *Education* really represents something of an introduction to the literary achievements of Joyce and Proust as well as to the behavioral science research of Perry and others. Joyce and Proust received the chaos of the modern world as a fixed condition and sought variously to express it and overcome it. Adams felt modernity as the outcome of a historical process through which he had lived and sought to register its development through a revision of his own experience. Fortunately for our purposes here, Adams shaped that revision around theologically resonant themes, such as creation and fall, spiritual recovery, and the contrast between human and divine powers.

Like Joyce in *A Portrait of the Artist,* Adams introduces the theme of creation and fall into the *Education* through the name of the work's central character. The name that Joyce invents for his alter ego in *A Portrait of the Artist,* Stephen Dedalus, signifies at once the name of the first Christian martyr and that of the great artificer of Greek mythology. Thus, Stephen Dedalus's name prefigures two of his major intellectual experiences: his struggle with the Catholic tradition and his discovery of his artistic vocation. In the *Education* the name Henry Adams has mythic implications of its own, invoking at one and the same time the heroic founding fathers of the American political tradition and the Biblical progenitor of all humankind. For many reasons, Adams adopted the peculiar narrative strategy of writing about himself in the third person. By repeating his own name throughout the *Education,* he suggests that the fate of America as well as the larger destiny of humanity can be figured in the fall of one Adams.

Adams figures the dramatic movement from innocence to failure to recovery by construing his education as a discontinuous series of efforts to regain the innocent and ordered world of the eighteenth century amid the chaos of the nineteenth and twentieth. The dominant motif of the *Education* is failure, an intellectual inability to find order in learning or experience coupled with a political failure to secure power over a world seemingly spun out of control. Recovery comes only with an act of usurpation: the self-styled victim of history eventually becomes its creator, and the failed political animal becomes the artist. The character Henry Adams finds only disorder, until he at last becomes the narrator who creates meaning through the medium of art that is the work itself. Creation is salvation. We are given finally the myth of the man-made self.

Adams's *Education* demonstrates that some reactions against the technological project—the remaking of the world through the application of scientific knowledge—can become themselves absorbed by the prospect of total mastery through creation. The fate of the figure Henry Adams in the hands of the author Henry Adams suggests that modern art and education, as well as modern technology, are driven by ambitions that are equally grandiose and finally idolatrous. We learn this by noting first how the *Education* identifies the figure of Adams with the fate of Western history; second how this Adams loses all sense of identity as a result of the pace of change; third how the *Education* ascribes change of any kind to the destructive, even demonic, effects of the technological project; and fourth how it presents the art of the *Education* itself as the saving remedy for Adams's fall from grace.

The narrator of the *Education* first insists that Henry Adams's experience is somehow commensurate with the American experience and then treats the American experience as the harbinger of the fate of the West. "Only with that understanding—as a consciously assenting member in full partnership with the society of his age—had his education an interest to himself or others," Adams the author wrote about Adams the figure.[15] Again and again, the narrator designates his central character simply as "the American."[16] Henry Adams's consciousness is America's consciousness. "America and he began, at the same time, to become aware of a new force under the innocent surface of party machinery."[17]

As Adams represents America, so America represents the fate of Western civilization, even of world history. When the young American, Henry Adams, goes to Rome in 1860, he finds only "conundrum after conundrum in his educational path, which seemed unconnected but that he had got to connect; that seemed insolvable but had got to be somehow resolved."[18] When he returns to the steps of the Roman church of Ara Coeli much later, he remembers his earlier visit, and he begins to fuse Rome and America.

> In forty years, America had made so vast a stride to empire that the
> world of 1860 stood already on a distant horizon somewhere on the

same plane with the republic of Brutus and Cato, while schoolboys read of Abraham Lincoln as they did of Julius Caesar. . . . The climax of empire could be seen approaching year after year, as though Sulla were a president or McKinley a Consul.[19]

What the young Henry Adams fails to connect the narrator pulls together in a compelling symbol of the American Henry Adams on the steps of the Ara Coeli contemplating the "Eternal City" of Western civilization. The marked contrast between the remembered Rome of 1860 and the Rome of 1900 images the speed of time. Sensing to his fingertips the pace of historical change around him, Adams makes the central figure of the *Education* a symbol of modern humanity overwhelmed by the velocity of history. The accelerating tempo of change since his birth, Adams realized, had again and again fractured the continuum of his life and had outrun his intellectual and emotional capacities. Indeed, the race of time had even made Adams an alien in his own land. "My country in 1900 is something totally different from my country of 1860. I am wholly a stranger in it."[20] The hapless hero of the *Education* constantly finds his life broken into fragments: "He was in a fair way to do himself lasting harm, floundering between worlds past and worlds coming, which had a habit of crushing men who stayed too long at the points of contact."[21] The most arresting images of the *Education* register a consciousness of change unparalleled in modern literature. When, for example, the Adamses return from England to the United States in 1868, the narrator says of them, "Had they been Tyrian traders of the year B.C. 1000, landing from a galley fresh from Gibraltar, they could hardly have been stranger on the shore of a world, so changed from what it had been ten years before."[22]

Adams believed that the force responsible for the vertiginous speed of history was technology. At once the glory and the curse of modern civilization, technology was fast outstripping the ability of human intelligence to control it, he feared. This worry ran through his letters from the 1860s to the end of his life. He warned his correspondents that human beings did not have "the mental powers to run such a vast and complicated machine."[23] In 1905, he told his brother, Brooks, that "man himself must make a big jump or break his neck. He must develop new mental powers or perish."[24] He made the antihero of the *Education* a victim of technological progress. The Cunard ocean liners, the telegraph, and the railroad separate him from his eighteenth-century world.[25] As a result of technological developments, he, "American of Americans, with Heaven knows how many Puritans and Patriarchs behind him, . . . was no worse off than the Indians or the buffalo who had been ejected from their own heritage by his own people. . . ."[26] Some new triumph of applied science—the steamship, the railroad, the dynamo, radium—marks each of the successive historical phases that confuse and overwhelm Adams and his education.

Indeed, *The Education of Henry Adams* constitutes the most sustained and searching meditation upon the social and psychological consequences of modern technological progress to emerge in the United States from the fin de siècle. The speedy advance of applied science, the *Education* suggests, threatens to obliterate forever humanity's consciousness of history. When the young Henry Adams visits Rome in 1860, the narrator remarks, "no sand blast of science had yet skinned off the epidermis of history, thought, and feeling."[27] By the end of the nineteenth century, however, the American mind "stood alone in history for its ignorance of the past."[28] Adams had grasped about his own period what the distinguished historian of fin de siècle Vienna grew to understand about modernism only after years of study and two generations of historical perspective:

> In a more complex way, emergent "modernism" has tended to take the specific form of what Heinz Kohut has called in another connection a "reshuffling of the self." Here historical change not only forces upon the individual a search for a new identity but also imposes upon whole social groups the task of revising or replacing defunct belief systems. The attempt to shake off the shackles of history has paradoxically speeded up the process of history, for indifference to any relationship with the past liberates the imagination to proliferate new forms and new constructs. Thus complex changes appear where once continuity reigned. Conversely, the consciousness of swift change in history-as-present weakens the authority of history as relevant past.[29]

If technology was the motor of modern civilization, science was its spirit, Adams maintained, and he believed that modern science vindicated his feelings about the world around him.[30] He compiled a notebook of quotations from scientists and philosophers of science, such as Karl Pearson, Arthur Balfour, Ernst Mach, Ernst Haeckel, and M. Poincaré.[31] All of these quotations supported the same conclusion: "Chaos was the law of nature; order the dream of man."[32] According to Adams's reading of the history of science, the rational, harmonious world of the ancients and the lawful, mathematical world of Newton and Darwin had given way to the unruly pluriverse of the twentieth century.

Modern scientists like Mach and Pearson had abandoned the Newtonian faith in the ultimate regularity of objective nature and had defined science as the disciplined effort of human beings to order subjective sense impressions. "Order and reason, beauty and benevolence," said Karl Pearson, "are characteristics and conceptions which we find solely associated with the mind of man."[33] Though Adams's understanding of the history and philosophy of science was incomplete, he surmised correctly that the focus of modern attention within the sciences as well as the arts had shifted away from external reality and back to the interior world of human consciousness. The best scientists and the best artists, Adams thought, could merely construct, through acts of imagination, a small and illusory world of sensual order from a universe of supersensual chaos.

These constructions were humanity's salvation from deformation. Adams's salvation came, then, not from his education but from his writing the *Education.* Toward the end of the book, the character Henry Adams resolves "to fix a position for himself, which he could label: *The Education of Henry Adams: A Study of Twentieth-Century Multiplicity.*"[34] Like Joyce's *A Portrait of the Artist* and Proust's *Remembrance of Things Past,* the *Education* is the story of its own creation. At the end of *A Portrait,* Stephen Dedalus discovers his vocation: "He would create proudly out of the freedom and power of his soul, as the great artificer whose name he bore, a living thing, new and soaring and beautiful, impalpable, imperishable."[35] Similarly, the character Marcel, the "I" of Proust's book, resolves at the end that he will write the story that the book has told. Adams, Joyce, and Proust all wrote books that are stories of their stories, works that describe the growth of a character into the narrative consciousness that in turn creates the work. In all of them, autobiography passes into a fictional account of the development of a distinctively modernist aesthetic sensibility. One critic's summary of Proust's achievement applies exactly to Adams's *Education:*

> He reached beyond autobiography toward the transformation of his life into the shape of a story that could convey his deepest sense of self. . . . By seeing his personal situation from outside as if it radiated a larger generalized narrative of loss and recovery, he transformed his failures into potential successes and his isolation into communication.[36]

But these transformations were seen by several of the modernists themselves to be works of the devil. Thus, Joyce's Stephen abjures his Christian heritage, adopting the motto of a defiant Lucifer, *Non serviam*, (I will not serve), as he embraces his artistic vocation.[37] Thus, Weber defends and advances the process of intellectualization as one who "hates intellectualism as the worst devil."[38] And thus, Adams fabricates himself and his world even as he knows such fabrications rest upon profound deceit. The American Adams has become the father of lies. Creation in Adams's hands is a form of deception. To some extent, the modernists could view these demonic undertakings ironically precisely *because* they could still rely upon their audience's knowledge of the very mythology they were subverting. Thus, Joyce could rely on his readers to know the fates of Lucifer and Icarus. Thus, too, Weber could rely upon his audience to be familiar with the Reformed and the Lutheran traditions. So too with Adams. Perhaps because he had not succeeded in completely expunging his Puritan conscience, Adams had ruefully to admit that "even when the mind existed in a universe of its own creation, it had never been quite at ease."[39] At least literary modernists like Adams, Joyce, and Proust were able to maintain some measure of ironic distance from the more grandiose ambitions of their alter egos.

However intricate the ironies, the theological significance of the *Education* arises from a clear transvaluation of spiritual values. The creature Adams registers the disappearance of his Creator by becoming the author of himself—both creator and authority. His wandering spirit seeks, not reunion or reconciliation with the divine, but further estrangement from both the divine and the human. In one sad, brave, wonderful book, Adams thereby charts the course of modern alienation by presenting one persona's repeatedly futile efforts to *discover* meaning in the world around him. Yet, the *Education* represents that very "formula of his own" by which its author *made* sense of his life to himself and to hundreds of modern readers after him. At least, Adams confessed, the *Education* had succeeded in educating him.

This "confession" articulates the quintessence of modernity: education is understood as a spiritual quest for meaning; this quest ends with its expression. Adams was right to represent himself as prototypically modern in this regard. Charles Taylor's recent, magisterial description of the modern identity demonstrates just how prescient Adams was.

To the extent that one sees the finding of a believable framework as the object of a quest, to that extent it becomes intelligible that the search might fail. This might happen through personal inadequacy, but failure might also come from there being no ultimately believable framework. Why speak of this in terms of a loss of meaning? Partly because a framework is that in virtue of which we make sense of our lives spiritually. Not to have a framework is to fall into a life which is spiritually senseless. The quest is thus always a quest for sense.

But the invocation of meaning also comes from our awareness of how much the search involves articulation. We find the sense of life through articulating it. And moderns have become acutely aware of how much sense being there for us depends on our own powers of expression. Discovering here depends on, is interwoven with, inventing. Finding a sense to life depends on framing meaningful expressions which are adequate.[40]

We have accordingly sought to comprehend the spiritual dimensions of the modernist understanding of education by attending to Adams's *expression* of it. A brief study of the relationship between Adams's intellectual life and his *Education* will reveal the sources of this modernist expression and so conclude our analysis. We shall postpone an assessment of its relative adequacy to the final chapter.

IV

Adams's life was stranger and more instructive than the fiction that he made of it. A brief rehearsal of that life and its relationship to the *Education* will review many of the issues that we have examined throughout the course of the present study of religion and the academic vocation in America. This reexamination will, however, add a new dimension to our analysis, for it will demonstrate, in the life of one human being at least, the inner logic of the movement from a faith in the settled verities of a tradition of civic and religious virtue to a commitment to objectivism to an identification of learning with making. Underlying these transformations we will discover a quest for knowledge as power in the face not only of a growing sense of impotence but also of a virtual disintegration of the self. In brief, an examination of Adams's life will reveal some of the psychic and spiritual stresses that accompanied and led to the emergence of modernity.

In order to secure our historical grasp upon the problem of the academic vocation, we must see how and why the logic of both *techne* and art became deeply connected, in the mind of one American at least, to a repudiation of community and the lonely pursuit of power. Our focus will therefore be upon two transformations: the movement from republican and religious virtues to the objectivism of positivist science and the movement from positivist science to modernist art. Along the way, we will encounter many by now familiar themes—the replacement of tradition by procedural rationality, the dangers of terminal wistfulness, the reorientation of piety from divine toward technological powers, the abandonment of a concern for character in favor of the cultivation of a multifaceted personality, and the sense of modern education as a movement in the opposite direction from the one taken in the *Confessions* of St. Augustine. If we avoid the temptation to overgeneralize, we really can learn something of our own current educational predicament by studying the life and education of one Adams.

The young Henry Adams was someone whom both Jeffrey Stout and Robert Bellah would have admired, someone for whom the religious virtues of a form of Biblical tradition really were continuous with the classically republican virtues of the early American experiment. When the narrator of the *Education* sought to recapture and dispel the child-hood fantasy that the unique accidents of one's own history are universal features of human experience, he turned naturally to images that combined the political with the religious. "It was unusual for boys to sit [in church] behind a President grandfather, and to read over his head the tablet in memory of a President great-grandfather, . . . but boys naturally supposed that other boys had the equivalent of President grandfathers and that churches would always go on, with the bald-headed leading citizens on the main aisle, and the Presidents or their equivalent on the walls."[41]

The young Henry Adams was utterly devoted to his family's faith in the God of a once vigorous but rapidly fading Puritanism and in the classical republican virtues of the eighteenth century. He absorbed these loyalties, not in terms of philosophical abstractions, but through the gestures and rituals by which the Adamses transmitted an intellectual inheritance over the generations: the cataloguing of the family library, the editing of presidential papers, the formal attire, the measured rhythms of speech, the early cultivation of a regular and carefully phrased correspondence. These rites of passage led easily to more formal schooling at two private preparatory schools before Henry entered

Harvard in 1854. There he further fortified his family tradition. The
curriculum at Harvard was inflexible, instruction was largely routine and
recitative, and the "prevailing pressure was, so to speak, from the
northeast, sternly conservative in all the 'moral sciences,' deeply Christian in its ethics, idealist in the drift of its philosophy. . . ."[42]
Whatever its considerable shortcomings measured by present standards,
this was the pre-Eliot Harvard that regarded character formation as
necessarily central to the mission of higher education.

In his old age, Adams attributed the dissipation of his imposing cultural inheritance in part to the waning of those religious affections that
had once inspired and sustained it. This attribution reminds us that the
positing of an alleged decline in religious piety has been a persistent
refrain in American culture, making the jeremiad a favorite American
genre. Adams's own retrospective statement is less alarmist than
ruefully bewildered:

> In uniform excellence of life and character, moral and intellectual, the
> score of Unitarian clergymen about Boston, who controlled society
> and Harvard College, were never excelled. They proclaimed as their
> merit that they insisted on no doctrine, but taught, or tried to teach, the
> means of leading a virtuous, useful, unselfish life, which they held to
> be sufficient for salvation. . . . Of all the conditions of his youth
> which afterwards puzzled the grown-up man, this disappearance of
> religion puzzled him most. The boy went to church every Sunday; he
> was taught to read his Bible, and he learned religious poetry by heart;
> he believed in a mild deism; he prayed; he went through all the forms;
> but neither to him nor to his brothers and sisters was religion real.
> Even the mild discipline of the Unitarian Church was so irksome that
> they all threw it off at the first possible moment, and never afterwards
> entered a church. The religious instinct had vanished and could not be
> revived, though one made in later life many efforts to recover it.[43]

Adams raises here the same quandary with which we closed Chapter 3,
namely, the worry over whether certain virtues can be sustained over
time absent the religious affections and practices that originally gave rise
to them. But the passage reports more than it explains Adams's own
abandonment of the life of public and religious virtue for scientific
study.

That momentous change took place during the American Civil War
when Henry found himself drawn to positivism in order to cope with his
growing sense of impotence and alienation. In 1861, he reluctantly left

the theater of action in the United States and accompanied his father, Charles Francis Adams, to England. President Lincoln had appointed the elder Adams to the most crucial diplomatic post of the war, ambassador to Great Britain, and Henry dutifully agreed to continue to serve as his father's private secretary, a post he had held during the previous several months in Washington. At first, Henry pleaded with his older brother, Charles, to secure an army commission for him, but he gradually resigned himself to his position of comparative ineffectuality. And the more he found himself withdrawn, the more he studied works of science, philosophy, and history. As he found himself removed from the immediate scene of events in the United States, so he became inclined to locate the causes of historical events at increasingly remote distances from their effects. He noted that those close to the conflict, like his brother, Charles, whose ears were "deafened" and whose eyes were "dazzled" by army parades, believed the outcome of the war would depend upon specific military engagements.[44] But English policy toward the Union, Henry insisted, would have little relation to the advances or retreats of armies. Instead, the English position on the naval blockade, for example, depended upon the "greater or less supply of cotton," upon agricultural developments in India and conditions in the world market.[45] Not individual effort or will, not incidental strategies or miscalculations, but impersonal economic and social forces determined the course of history, Adams began to suspect. His vision repelled him: "The only thing that disgusts me much is the consciousness that we are unable to govern [the world], the condition that a man of sense can only prove his possession of a soul by remaining in mind a serene and indifferent spectator to the very events to which his acts most eagerly contribute."[46]

Here was a clear statement, in the context of social and political alienation, of what Parker Palmer would later call "objectivism." For Henry Adams, serenity and indifference to the world and a corresponding detachment from community did not come easily. Indeed, despite his frustrations in England, he continued for several years after his return to the United States in 1868 to seek to manage the course of political events through his writing and counsel. He continued to believe that a certain type of intelligence would guarantee or at least should guarantee social and political influence, that ideas shaped reality, not vice versa. All of these efforts proved unavailing, however, so Adams steadily abandoned his quest for a practical science of politics and turned toward the further study of scientific history. In both cases, Adams sought knowledge for the sake of power, but he shifted from an effort to make history through principled and heroic political action to an effort to *make* history by writing it.

The turn toward objectivism and *Wissenschaft* took place within a particular institutional and epistemic context. In 1870, Harvard's new president, Eliot, invited Adams to join him in transforming Harvard from the provincial college it had been into a modern university that promoted research and experiment. Adams had already absorbed the positivist principles of explanation that would inform his own scholarship. In England, he had been especially taken with the tenth edition of Charles Lyell's *Principles of Geology,* especially with Lyell's forceful argument, against Cuvier and other "catastrophists," that the geological record had developed over millions of years according to the steady and uniform action of the same causal forces of wind, water, and temperature that prevailed in Lyell's own time. Adams had in turn speculated that nations developed according to the same "process" that was "evident in the ocean and the air. . . ."[47] And he predicted that "the laws which govern animated beings will be ultimately found to be at the bottom the same with those which rule inanimate nature. . . ."[48] The burgeoning research university and the objectivist epistemology, Adams found, were mutually reinforcing.

For our purposes at the moment, however, the spiritual dimensions of Adams's objectivism are more important than the cultural and institutional ones. For roughly twenty years after he accepted his Harvard appointment, Adams subjected himself to the rigors of an academic discipline that promised scientific mastery but that was finally *self*-defeating. For most of that period Adams worked on what eventually became his nine-volume *History of the United States during the Administrations of Thomas Jefferson and James Madison.* In writing it, he sought to advance the cause of scientific history by undercutting the great-man theory of historical change and demonstrating that democracies developed according to impersonal laws. The human mind, Adams tried to show, was fundamentally powerless to shape history, because the converse was also true: power was fundamentally mindless, developing always according to abstract mechanical forces.

Adams's favorite device for demonstrating this truth was his knowingly ironic treatment of Thomas Jefferson, the tragicomic hero of the *History* with whom, of all the figures in the work, Adams most closely identified himself.[49] As Adams portrayed him, Jefferson never seemed to grasp his own inevitable impotence, and he remained forever convinced of the efficacy of his democratic ideals. Adams's interpretation undercut this naive faith at every turn. He relished showing how Jefferson was repeatedly compelled to act against his own best intentions. "Not by means of government, or by virtue of the wisdom in the persons trusted with government," Adams derisively observed, "were Jefferson's objects at last to be partially achieved."[50] Again and again, Adams demonstrated that Jefferson's leadership was at worst counterproductive and at best superfluous. Democracies, he insisted, developed through mechanical and unconscious processes, not through human thought and will. Jefferson had therefore inaugurated a system of government that made him distressingly irrelevant. And Adams, in writing the *History,* had proved, to his own satisfaction at least, that serving historical science was the only sensible way to *make* history, that scholarship and not politics was the only viable pursuit for the intellectual in a democratic society.

Though the *History* did manage to justify Adams's own occupation in writing it, it did so at enormous spiritual cost. Self-effacement was the price of avoiding self-deception, thereby retaining a measure of control over the historical world. In his *Education,* Adams claimed that "he never got to the point of playing the game [of life] at all; he *lost himself* in the study of it, watching the errors of the players. . . ."[51] The image of life as a game and the persona Henry Adams as a spectator might stem here from the Greek root of the word *theory* [*theoria*], which was used to describe the activity of a spectator at an athletic contest. In any event, the image of himself as a "serene and indifferent spectator" was one that Adams used regularly for over forty years. Yet even as he withdrew further and further from the world of public affairs, even as he sought to cultivate in his historical writing a style of scrupulous impersonality, Adams realized that objectivism was spiritually fatal to him. He had referred from the beginning to "geology and science" as his *"burial place* of ambition. . . ."[52] And he noted with ironic appreciation the double entendre in Karl Pearson's word for objectivism. Both good citizens and good scientists, Pearson insisted, needed to practice "self-elimination" in their judgments.[53] Adams used a double entendre that made a similar point in his *History:* "The interest of [democracy] exceeded that of any other branch of science," he wrote, "for it brought mankind within the sight of his own end."[54] The logic of objectivism and the language of spiritual suicide were closely bound up with one another in the vocabulary of Adams and several of his contemporaries.

Adams the historian had grown remarkably like Joyce's artist, Stephen Dedalus. Both had discovered vocations in the process of leaving religion and public life behind them. Both had therefore embraced their callings by moving away from community, not toward it. Adams, influenced in part by the ethos of the modern university, had adopted a conception of the discipline of scientific history that removed all evidence of the author from the work itself. Joyce's Stephen settled upon an aesthetic, borrowed from the great French realist Flaubert, that called for the artist to be icily remote from his work, utterly disengaged, "paring his fingernails." To arrive fully at the position of Joyce, it remained only for Adams to turn the detached perspective of his *History* upon himself, an achievement that he managed, as we have seen, when he composed his own "autobiography" entirely in the third person.

The way to the latter accomplishment led, for Adams, to the great Gothic cathedrals of France, and beyond them to an experience of terminal wistfulness so powerful that it drove his efforts to recover a "vanished religious instinct" to bizarre but instructive extremities. Perhaps because he had found the practice of positivist history such cheerless therapy for his growing sense of impotence, he did not, with one minor exception, write history again from 1890, when he finished his *History,* to his death in 1918. He began instead an extensive program of travel to the South Sea islands and the Orient, to Paris and the surrounding French countryside, to the southern Mediterranean and the Near East, and to Cuba and the vast interior of the North American continent. Though he had always been afflicted with wanderlust, he had thought it "ludicrous to play Ulysses." But in 1890, when he left the United States for a South Sea voyage, he took a copy of the *Odyssey* with him. He was in truth leaving this time on a mission, seeking some place in the world of past or present where he could finally feel at home. Ulysses had at last become a suitable traveling companion for him.[55]

Adams's quest seemed complete, when he stood before the Gothic cathedrals. In expressions as powerful as they were uncanny, he registered repeatedly his conviction that he himself had created them. "Caen, Bayeux, St. Lo, Coutances, and Mont St. Michel are clearly works I helped to build, when I lived in a world I liked. . . . With true Norman work, the sensation is that of personal creation."[56] Again, to another close friend, "I am sure that in the eleventh century the majority of me was Norman, . . . and that by some chance I did not share the actual movement of the world but became a retarded development, and unable to find a place.''[57] Sentiments like these suggest that Adams's wistfulness amounted to a "shock of recognition," an ineffable feeling that he saw himself in the works of art before him.

These experiences eventually led to the publication, in 1913, of *Mont St. Michel and Chartres.* The book offered a sweeping and highly personal view of the meaning of medieval culture, an interpretation that was fortified by considerable scholarship to be sure, but one that issued mainly from its author's imagination. Written in a densely metaphorical style, *Mont St. Michel and Chartres* explored medieval poetry, art, architecture, and philosophy as concrete expressions of the spirit of a civilization. But the book was not an academic treatise; rather, Adams managed to represent in it a period and a place that could serve as the dwelling place of his own spirit, thereby rendering in prose an iconography of his own emotions. Indeed, to some extent the artifacts of the Middle Ages that Adams selected for study really did symbolize several furtive qualities of his consciousness: heroism, awe, a sense of mystery, piety, and romantic love. Thus the tone of the work, as uncanny as that of the letters quoted earlier, made it seem as though he had some privileged access to the inner meaning of the objects he described. "We are not," he cautioned his readers, "studying grammar or archaeology, and would rather be inaccurate in such matters than not, if, at that price, a freer feeling of the art could be caught."[58]

All of this, however understandable it might have been, represented yet another form of withdrawal from the world, this time in the name of art rather than science. Thus, *Mont St. Michel and Chartres* contained the sort of cultural criticism that is vulnerable to Stoutian charges of terminal wistfulness. Much of this was not original with Adams. Scores of nineteenth-century writers, especially English Pre-Raphaelites like William Morris, had extolled the craftsmanship, art, and spiritual unity of medieval culture as a sort of anodyne for the crassness of modern civilization.[59] The most concise statement of what became Adams's own variant of this theme came immediately after he first studied the Gothic cathedrals in 1895:

I have rarely felt New England at its highest ideal power as it appeared to me, beautified and glorified, in the cathedral of Coutances. Since then our ancestors have declined steadily and run out until we have

> reached pretty near bottom. . . . They have lost their religion, their
> art and their military tastes. They cannot now comprehend the mean-
> ing of what they did at Mont St. Michel. They have kept only the
> qualities which were most useful, with a dull instinct recalling dead
> associations. So we get Boston.[60]

Adams sometimes explained others' lack of appreciation for his work by
reiterating this kind of cultural criticism. Modern human beings would
not understand *Mont St. Michel and Chartres,* he claimed, because they
could not understand it. Hence, his contemporaries' lack of understanding merely confirmed a central argument of the book itself: moderns
were devoid of aesthetic and religious sensibilities.[61]

Because Adams circulated the text of *Mont St. Michel and Chartres* to
a very few people, his statements about the poverty of feeling among his
contemporaries represented at best a kind of self-fulfilling cultural criticism. Overwhelmed, as he was, by a somewhat belated and therefore all
the more intense emotional awakening, he made the mistake common to
many who have had such experiences: he believed that he was the *only*
person, or at most one of a select few, capable of such feelings. This
conviction led him at times to relish his isolation and to make remarks
about the place of the artist in society that have a distinctly neo-
Romantic and therefore modern ring to them. "As my experience leads
me to think that no one any longer cares or even knows what is said or
printed," Adams wrote, "and one's audience in history and literature
has shrunk to a mere band of survivors, not exceeding a thousand people
in the entire world, I am in hopes a kind of esoteric literary art will
survive, the freer and happier for the sense of privacy and *abandon."*[62]
This advocacy of an "esoteric literary art" as well as the association of
artistic freedom with the withdrawal of art from the public to the private
realm have recurred as themes in the lives of several twentieth-century
writers. The conception of art as a necessarily cryptic enterprise has
appealed to many of them, not only because of its elitist overtones, but
also because the conception subtly transforms a sociological fact into a
normative principle. If art is made into an intricate cipher for the cogno-
scenti, the writer's feeling of alienation from society becomes a test of
his or her artistic integrity.

We have thus seen in Henry Adams not one but two forms of what
Weber would later call "worldly asceticism." The first one was academic, the second artistic. The first was informed by an objectivist

epistemology affiliated with science and technology and devoted to *Wissenschaft;* the second by a modernist aesthetic accompanied by terminal wistfulness and devoted, like its academic counterpart, to the activity of making as the summum bonum. Both regarded education, construed primarily in terms of making, as a way of gaining a greater measure of power and control over self and world. And both insisted that the practice of vocation must be a lonely, even an alienating, business.

These twin ambitions and their interconnections have become even more pronounced and extreme in our own time. So, for example, Richard Rorty, whose earlier work stressed, as we have seen, the social dimension of thought, has turned more recently to the avowedly neo-Romantic celebration of the individual bravely "inventing new vocabularies."[63] Like many other thinkers of our generation, Rorty has announced that literary and cultural criticism are really art forms. They too are forms of making; they too invent the new. Rorty's endeavors here are but a small part of a much larger movement embracing thinkers in many academic disciplines who claim for themselves and their disciplines the vocation of remaking the world. Though this development is at times both dreadful and pathetic, it should not surprise us, given the psychological and social affiliations between the two forms of worldly asceticism that we have seen so clearly dramatized in the life of Henry Adams.

Add to the similarities between these two forms of worldly asceticism the displacement of piety from divine to technological powers, and we have before us a striking outline of the modern educated personality. In Adams's own terms, this shift in the objects of adoration meant a movement from the medieval world of the Virgin to the twentieth-century world of the Dynamo. "As he grew accustomed to the great gallery of the dynamos," Adams recollects his experience at the Paris Exposition of 1900, "he began to feel the forty-foot dynamos as a moral force, much as the early Christians felt the Cross. . . . Before the end, one began to pray to [the dynamo]; inherited instinct taught the natural expression of man before silent and infinite force."[64] The piety that might have sensed truly the spiritual power of the Virgin was "unknown to the American mind."[65] Instead, that religious affection had become, in a figure like the sculptor Augustus St. Gaudens, wholly aestheticized or, in a figure like Henry Adams, wholly scientized. "Each had but half of a nature, and when they came together before the Virgin of Amiens they ought both to have felt in her the force that made them one; but it

was not so. To Adams she became more than ever a channel of force; to
St. Gaudens she remained as before a channel of taste.''[66] The religious
affection that would have ''made them one'' had atrophied; thus, force
and beauty had become forever separated in apprehension as well as in
fact. As the poet Octavio Paz has well observed in his fine essay in praise
of handicrafts, much of modern industrial technology has given us function without beauty, and much of modern art has given us beauty
without function.[67]

Adams's contemplation of figures like Gibbon, St. Gaudens, and
Ruskin standing before the great cathedrals was a way of multiplying
perspectives, of distancing himself further and further from his subject,
and so of disintegrating the self. His life and the fiction that he made of it
in *The Education of Henry Adams* converge completely on the point of
lost identity. Thus, the detached narrator of the *History* appears as a
character in the ''Dynamo and the Virgin'' chapter of the *Education*.[68]
Yet this Henry Adams seems strangely different from the many other
Henry Adamses who appear as characters in the work—Henry Adams
''the child,'' Henry Adams ''the student,'' Henry Adams the private
secretary, journalist, Darwinian, voyager, poet.[69] To complicate matters still further, the narrator of the *Education* seems continuous and at
the same time discontinuous with all of these Henry Adamses. And the
sense of alienation from the self can be pressed to almost infinite regres-
sion, as we get passages that record the narrator Henry Adams watching
the character Henry Adams watching himself watch others as they stand
before the strange monument that marks his wife's grave.[70]

Thus both the *Education* and the life of its author present to us a
deeply unsettling portrait of fragmented consciousness in a world of
multiplicity. Unlike the *History,* which progresses in a smooth and
steady sequence of development, the *Education* lurches from one complex installment to another, sometimes skipping several years altogether.[71] The work is filled with awkward transitions and abrupt rever-
sals. Sentences, paragraphs, and chapters seem oddly disconnected.
This disjointed style formulates the discontinuous consciousness of both
author and protagonist. In a typical passage, the narrator describes
Henry Adams's feelings upon returning from Italy to England in 1865:

> He saw before him a world so changed as to be beyond connection
> with the past. His identity, if one could call a bundle of disconnected
> memories an identity, seemed to remain; but his life was once more

broken into separate pieces; he was a spider and had to spin a new web in some new place with a new attachment.[72]

Again, more tersely, "Adams's life, past or future, was a succession of violent breaks or waves, with no base at all."[73]

All of this is, in truth, an inversion of Augustine's *Confessions* and therefore of the paradigmatic spiritual autobiography of Western Christendom. Gene Koretz has noted structural and thematic parallels between Augustine's work and the *Education,* such as the use of symbolic episodes, the combination of narrative and didactic motives, and the concluding theoretical expositions.[74] But Adams developed the parallels for the purposes of heightening the contrast. Augustine writes the *Confessions* from the first-person perspective, speaking with the retrospective clarity, self-assurance, and commitment of a convert. Adams's narrator is like a cubist painter, often representing his material from several different views at once. "Time and experience," he writes, "alter all perspectives," and so on almost every page of the *Education,* the narrator, through elaborate tense shifts, presents a multiperspectival vision of the world.[75]

There is, moreover, a tremendous difference between Augustine's closing meditations on memory, time, and eternity and Adams's "Dynamic Theory of History" and "Law of Acceleration." Augustine celebrates the memory as the thread of personal identity, the bearer of the mystery of continuity. And he journeys more and more deeply into the interior of his soul believing that he will there find his Maker. Adams journeys farther and farther into the exterior, believing that he will find some standpoint from which he will frame a cosmic generalization that will "finish his clamor to be educated." Augustine praises; Adams seeks final solutions. Augustine believes in order to understand. Adams fails to understand, because he cannot believe.

The final chapters of the *Education* are a strange synthesis of metaphor and scientific theory, having roughly the same intellectual standing as Yeats's elaborate gyre theories. Adams half believed these sweeping cosmic pronouncements, and he half disbelieved them. Like the hero of his *Education,* he really did in his old age study economics, history, art, chemistry, physics, mathematics, politics, and philosophy to see whether any of them succeeded in "running order through chaos, direction through space, discipline through freedom, unity through multiplicity."[76] And again, like his protagonist, he ended his searches "driven to madness by the complexities and multiplicities of his new world."[77] Augustine found his Maker as his Maker found him; Adams, as we have seen, found that he had to become his own maker. It was at best a precarious achievement: the man-made self soon dissolved into a potentially infinite multiplicity of roles, masks, poses, and styles.

But however precarious it was, it complemented Weber's achievement almost perfectly. Weber took the academicians from *Bildung* to *Wissenschaft*, from the formation of character to the making of knowledge. Adams took students from the forging of identity to the multiplication of personae, from character to personality. Behind all of these vast cultural transformations, registered in the contrast between Adams and Augustine, lay one insistent, theological question: Who made us? To conclude our present inquiry, we must reconsider that question anew, this time by returning as exiles, temporarily and figuratively, to Eden.

Notes

1. Hannah Arendt, *The Human Condition* (The University of Chicago Press: Chicago, 1958), 153–59, 294–96.

2. William G. Perry, Jr., "Cognitive and Ethical Growth: The Making of Meaning," in A. W. Chickering, ed., *The Modern American College* (Jossey-Bass: San Francisco, 1981), 76–116.

3. *Forms of Intellectual and Ethical Development in the College Years* (Holt, Rinehart and Winston: New York, 1970).

4. "Cognitive and Ethical Growth," 80–82.

5. *Ibid.*, 83–89.

6. *Ibid.*, 90–97.

7. *Ibid.*, 97.

8. *Ibid.*, 107.

9. *Ibid.*

10. George Otto Trevelyan, the English historian, praised Adams's *Education*, because he thought it captured the England of his youth better than any other work he had read. Henry's brother, Charles Francis Adams, Jr., liked it, because it evoked the quality of his youth in Quincy. Bernard Berenson claimed that all New Englanders would read the work with an interest "nearly autobiographical." The letters that report these reactions are in the Henry Adams Papers and the Henry Cabot Lodge Papers at the Massachusetts Historical Society. The account of Adams's life and work told here is based upon my unpublished Ph.D. thesis, "The Making of Modern Consciousness in America: The Works and Careers of Henry Adams and William James" (Stanford University, 1978). I discuss reactions to the *Education* more extensively there in chapter 5, 123–26.

11. See, for example, Vern Wagner, *The Suspension of Henry Adams* (Wayne State University Press: Detroit, 1969); John J. Conder, *A Formula of His Own: Henry Adams's Literary Experiment* (University of Chicago Press: Chicago, 1970); and Melvin Lyon, *Symbol and Idea in Henry Adams* (University of Nebraska Press: Lincoln, 1970).

12. Harry Levin, *James Joyce: A Critical Introduction* (New Directions Books: Norfolk, Conn., 1941), 41.

13. *Ibid.*

14. Henry Adams to Whitelaw Reid (September 13, 1908), in Harold Dean Cater, ed., *Henry Adams and His Friends* (Houghton Mifflin: Boston, 1947), 623.

15. *The Education of Henry Adams,* Ernest Samuels, ed. (Houghton Mifflin: Boston, 1973), 4.

16. *Ibid.,* 235, 238, *passim.*

17. *Ibid.,* 48.

18. *Ibid.,* 90.

19. *Ibid.,* 367.

20. Henry Adams to Charles Milnes Gaskell (March 29, 1900), in Worthington C. Ford, ed., *The Letters of Henry Adams,* 2 vols. (Houghton Mifflin: Boston, 1930–38), 2:280.

21. *Education,* 83. Several times in the *Education,* Henry Adams's life is "broken in halves," 209, 294, 317.

22. *Ibid.,* 237.

23. Henry Adams to Elizabeth Cameron, Henry Adams Papers, Massachusetts Historical Society (July 9, 1915).

24. Henry Adams to Brooks Adams, Henry Adams Papers, Houghton Library (July 11, 1905).

25. *Education,* 5.

26. *Ibid.,* 238.

27. *Ibid.,* 90.

28. *Ibid.,* 328.

29. Carl E. Schorske, *Fin-de-Siècle Vienna* (Random House: New York, 1981), xvlli.

30. As we will see subsequently, Adams used selected theories from the natural sciences to structure a positivist philosophy of history. But he could at the same time use science in a different and in some respects an opposite way. Any given scientific theory might be used to order nature and history, Adams believed, but he also argued that the philosophy of modern science increasingly asserted that chaos, not order, was the ultimate truth of nature.

31. The notebook is in the Henry Adams Papers, 1890 Box, Massachusetts Historical Society. The book is undated, but Adams must have copied the quotations in it between 1900 and 1905, because many of the sources that he

copied date from those years. Several of the entries in the notebook appear verbatim in chapter 31 of the *Education*, "The Grammar of Science (1903)," 449–61.

32. *Education*, 451.

33. Pearson quoted by Adams, *Education*, 450. The quotation also appears in the notebook described in n. 31.

34. *Education*, 435.

35. James Joyce, *A Portrait of the Artist as a Young Man* (Viking Press: New York, 1968), 170.

36. Roger Shattuck, *Marcel Proust* (Viking Press: New York, 1974), 149.

37. *A Portrait*, 164.

38. Max Weber, "Science as a Vocation," in H. H. Gerth and C. Wright Mills, trans. and eds., *From Max Weber: Essays in Sociology* (Oxford University Press: New York, 1977), 152.

39. *Education*, 460.

40. Charles Taylor, *Sources of the Self: The Making of the Modern Identity* (Harvard University Press: Cambridge, 1989), 17–18.

41. *Education*, 15–16.

42. Ernest Samuels, *The Young Henry Adams* (Harvard University Press: Cambridge, 1948), 30.

43. *Education*, 34.

44. Henry Adams, "From London," *New York Times,* July 14, 1861, 2. Adams could argue the opposite position with equal vigor, and he stated more than once that a Union victory would do more than anything else to increase English public sentiment for the North.

45. *Ibid.*

46. Henry Adams to Charles Francis Adams, Jr. (October 30, 1863), in Worthington C. Ford, ed., *A Cycle of Adams Letters, 1861–1865,* 2 vols. (Houghton Mifflin: Boston, 1920), 2:97.

47. Henry Adams to Charles Francis Adams, Jr., *Cycle,* 2:90 (October 2, 1863).

48. *Ibid.*

49. Adams was recognized by his students at Harvard during the 1870s as a partisan of Thomas Jefferson. The affinities between the two men extended to the politics of Liberal Reform and beyond them to matters of temperament, social situation, and personal appearance. Both Jefferson as president and Henry Adams as a Liberal Reformer in the post–Civil War period sought to restrict federal interference in social and economic affairs. Jefferson, the "aristocrat as democrat," as Adams ironically and empathetically called him, appeared shy, diffident, awkward, even cold, to many observers, just as Adams himself did.

50. Henry Adams, *History of the United States during the Administrations of Thomas Jefferson and James Madison*, 9 vols. (Charles Scribner's Sons: New York, 1889–91), 3:348.

51. *Education*, 4.

52. Henry Adams to Charles Francis Adams, Jr., *Letters*, 1:95 (February 20, 1863).

53. *The Grammar of Science* (A. and C. Black: London, 1900), 6–8 ff.

54. *History*, 9:225.

55. Ernest Samuels, *Henry Adams: The Major Phase* (Harvard University Press: Cambridge, 1964), 17, 108.

56. Henry Adams to John Hay, *Henry Adams and His Friends*, 346 (September 7, 1895).

57. Henry Adams to Charles Milnes Gaskell, *Letters*, 2:79 (September 1, 1895).

58. Henry Adams, *Mont St. Michel and Chartres* (Doubleday: New York, 1959), 18.

59. Samuels, *Henry Adams: The Major Phase*, 212–13.

60. Henry Adams to Brooks Adams, *Letters*, 2:80 (September 8, 1895).

61. The attitude expressed in the following letter is typical: "As our society stands, this way of presenting a subject [Adams's way in *Mont St. Michel and Chartres*] can be felt only by a small number of persons. My idea is that the world outside—the so-called modern world—can only pervert and degrade the conceptions of the primitive instinct of art and feeling, and that our only chance is to accept the limited number of survivors—the one-in-a-thousand of born artists and poets—and to intensify the energy of feeling within that radiant center." Henry Adams to Albert S. Cook, *Letters*, 2:546–7 (August 6, 1910).

62. Henry Adams to Charles Milnes Gaskell, *Letters*, 2:476 (May 10, 1907).

63. This unabashed and fervid celebration of the neo-Romantic strain in modernism begins at the very beginning of Rorty's most recent book and continues unabated throughout. As but one of the more disturbing illustrations of the pathetic consequences of this immoderate enthusiasm, I offer Rorty's praise of an obscene fantasy composed by Jacques Derrida that portrays Plato and Socrates in pornographic detail. Rorty interprets this bizarre Derridean indulgence as evidence that Derrida has freed himself completely from the philosophical tradition and has thereby achieved absolute autonomy. *Contingency, Irony, and Solidarity* (Cambridge University Press: Cambridge, 1989), 3; 128, 137.

64. *Education*, 380.

65. *Ibid.*, 385.

66. *Ibid.*, 387.

67. Octavio Paz, "In Praise of Hands," *Atlantic* 233 (May, 1974), 45–52.

68. *Education*, 382.

69. The narrator of the *Education* often refers to Henry Adams, the figure-mannikin, simply in terms of one of his many roles, e.g., "the young reformer of thirty" or "the student of history," *ibid.*, 245, 453.

70. *Ibid.*, 329.

71. For example, the *Education* skips from chapter 20, "Failure (1871)," to chapter 21, "Twenty Years After (1892)."

72. *Education*, 209.

73. *Ibid.*, 312.

74. "Augustine's *Confessions* and *The Education of Henry Adams*," *Comparative Literature* 3 (Summer, 1960), 205.

75. *Education*, 25.

76. *Ibid.*, 12.

77. *Ibid.*, 395.

6

Conclusion: Adam's Exile

I

"In Adam's fall/ We sinned all." This ditty from the *New England Primer* belongs quite literally to the alphabet of early American schooling. Its theology belongs ultimately to Augustine, the author of the doctrine of original sin. But what became, for centuries after Augustine, one of the orthodox teachings of Western Christendom became for Henry Adams, the self-styled fallen American, a mere conceit, a presumptuous play upon a name. By subverting the Protestant ethic, Max Weber, Adams's exact contemporary, formulated the modern academic ethos. By inverting the Augustinian version of the Christian story, Adams developed a beguiling image of the modern educated personality.

I have tried in this essay to explore the considerable historical significance of these subversions. To read Max Weber is to understand the utterly distinctive character of the modern research university as itself the result of those forces of modernity that Weber analyzed as acutely and extensively as anyone else in the twentieth century. To read Henry Adams, feeling with profound ambivalence these same abstract forces of specialization, intellectualization, and disenchantment, is to witness the creation of the modern university graduate. Indeed, as I have tried to show here, Adams's *Education* represents something of a modern manual of spiritual development from unity to multiplicity, from innocent wonder to "committed contextual relativism."

127

We have seen that Weber defined the modern academic vocation by transmuting a religious vocabulary drawn from the Reformed tradition. We have therefore reappropriated from the Reformed and from other religious traditions the language of the spiritual virtues to develop an alternative account of the academic calling. This redescription permitted us to see that many contemporary practices within the academy still depend for their success upon the exercise of the very spiritual virtues that the prevalent Weberian ethos would deny or obscure from view.

In a manner and with a purpose very much like Weber's, Henry Adams and James Joyce appropriated and sometimes subverted the mythic vocabulary of the great Biblical creation narratives in order to develop distinctively modern expressions of spiritual formation. But how can we assess the relative adequacy of these modernist formulations? We should, I think, at least begin such an assessment (and the ending of this book can deliver nothing more than just such a beginning) by asking whether Adams's *Education* is truly superior to the account of Adam's education in the book of Genesis as a diagnosis of the modern human condition. In other words, as we did with Weber, we will now critically appraise the modernist myth of education by comparing it to the very myth that it sought to subvert and replace.

In Genesis 1:27 we are told that the male and the female were created in the image of God. Volumes have been written over the centuries in an effort to explain the meaning of the *imago dei*. Whatever the full implications of the idea might be, one interpretation seems clear from the text and from the most persistent of the traditions of reading it. Human beings were meant to share in the creative powers of their Maker. We therefore cannot discount altogether the modernist emphasis upon *homo faber*, and we surely want to preserve what is both truthful and important in the notion that humankind participates most fully in the divine in the act of creation. On the other hand, the first creation story makes it quite clear that the Creator, not the human creatures, gives form to matter, animation to dust, order to chaos. The Orderer and the activity of ordering precede humanity.

The second creation narrative provides the basic materials from which the various modernist myths have been fashioned and refashioned. The earth creature, the *ha'adam,* of this second creation story, belongs, given the dynamics of modernity as I have described them in the previous chapter, to all of us in the contemporary West, whether or not we are religious. We will therefore all experience, as we retrieve some of the insights in the story of the first Adam, something of a shock of recognition. Precisely because so many of the emphases in the story have been strangely inverted over the course of the last century, the authority, the power, and the truth of the original story seem now, ironically enough, all the more compelling. Its authority derives, for the religious and the nonreligious alike, not from ecclesiastical imprimaturs, still less from divine decree, but from the immanent powers of the text to disclose to us our own condition. As we grow more deeply aware of the predicaments of our century, the original myth seems to set before us the truth about ourselves more thoroughly and persuasively than any of its modernist variants.

If we read this second creation narrative as a philosophical exploration of the human condition expressed in narrative form, we will find that it speaks directly to at least three of the central matters that occupied Henry Adams and that have occupied us throughout this book. We shall accordingly address, by way of conclusion, each of these three interrelated issues in turn: the quest for community, the perilous pursuit of knowledge as power, and the point of education in a disordered world.

II

The Quest for Community

Immediately after the Lord God has spoken for the first time to the earth creature, the human taken from the ground, the Creator concludes that it is *not* good that this creature should be alone in the world. The first speaking in this story creates or at least makes manifest the condition of creatureliness: God commands, the human listens; God permits and prohibits, setting limits for the human. In other words, Creator and creature are not equal, not perhaps fitting companions. Whatever the case here, human loneliness arises as a problem immediately after the creature becomes aware that it *is* a creature, that it is in a very direct and explicit sense limited.

The Lord God instantly discerns this difficulty and moves to remedy it, soon enlisting the counsel and aid of the earth creature in the process. The Lord God creates the animals, bringing them before the earth creature "to see what he would name them." Thus, language, the power to name and classify; judgment, the capacity to determine what is fit for companionship and what is not; and co-creation, the authority to dispose of what the Lord God proposes, arise in the quest for community. The new human vocabulary of classification does not *create* being where there was none before; rather, it determines relationship in the course of conferring identity. Inventing a vocal index here is most definitely not a desperate gesture of *origin*ality. And indeed, human beings still name and classify animals, including especially the fossilized remains of early hominids, with reference to themselves and to the relationships that are thought to obtain between any given animal species and the genus *Homo*.

Alas, after all of the animals are formed (like the human "out of the ground"), "there was not found a helper fit" for human companionship. Radical surgery seems required. And so the Creator creates once more, not one but two new beings—the human male and the human female. Out of one, the earth creature, come two, man and woman. This reading is a matter of considerable scholarly controversy, and I have on this latter point relied upon Phyllis Trible for the argument that the earth creature was, according to the Genesis 2 account, originally sexually undifferentiated (neither male nor female nor a combination of both). I will only note in passing that if we turn to embryology rather than to mythology for guidance in these matters, we find some peculiar affinities between Trible's reading of Genesis 2:21–24 and contemporary scientific accounts of how human life begins and develops in utero. Here, for example, is Stephen J. Gould on the embryological development of gender: "The external differences between male and female develop gradually from an early embryo so generalized that its sex cannot be easily determined. . . . Males and females are not separate entities, shaped independently by natural selection. Rather the two sexes are variants upon a single ground plan, elaborated in later embryology."[1]

The point here is not to look to embryology or, as earlier, to the practices of paleographers in order to establish, through exegetical legerdemain, the "truth" of the Genesis story. The point is rather to demonstrate the philosophical probity of the account regarding the relationship between the exercise of reason and the creation of community. Community is *finally* accomplished through an act of acknowledgment: "This at last is bone of my bones and flesh of my flesh." The last word of Genesis 2 is a later interpolation that seeks to construe both physical intimacy and generation as signs of this acknowledgment over time.

"Therefore a man leaves his father and mother and cleaves to his wife, and they become one flesh."

Though some of these readings have occasioned considerable controversy, three points, at least, seem indisputable from a reading of Genesis 2. First, the human exercises discriminating judgment in order to establish and secure relationships. Second, this endeavor takes place within a context of harmony between the human and the divine, the vegetable world and the animal world. Third, the male and the female are indeed "variants upon a single ground plan," grounded, if you will, in a common humanity itself formed "from the ground" by a creator God who seeks to remedy human loneliness through the creation of gender and companionship. The principal source of attraction between the sexes is loneliness, not erotic desire. Finally, knowledge and acknowledgment are linked to intimacy and community, not to alienation and estrangement. The exercise of discernment arises here in quest of community and later in the very act of procreation. Human beings as here portrayed are more pro-creators than co-creators.

Knowledge as Power

In Genesis 2, we find only harmony, equality, and community. The man and the woman stand "naked" and "not ashamed" before their Creator. But already by Genesis 3:7, the man and the woman are naked and ashamed. Then, in Genesis 3:16, the Creator tells the woman, "your desire shall be for your husband, and he shall rule over you." Innocence and community have given way to self-consciousness and domination. The transition from the one state to the other, from Eden to human culture, is the partial result of the pursuit of knowledge as a form of power.

More exactly, humankind's "first disobedience," as Milton called it, involves the illicit grasp of knowledge in order to become divine. The serpent introduces the interrogative mode into paradise. Questions. The woman answers, thinks critically, judges, misjudges, sees, hungers, seeks wisdom, aspires to deity. Grasps. Eats. Violates limits. Disobeys. So far as we can tell, the man participates fully with her in this extremely complicated process: "She took of its fruit and ate; and she also gave some to her husband, and he ate." The narrative here defies reduction to any simple doctrinal formulation about *the* fundamental character of or motive for human disobedience. The lust of the eyes may well be involved, as St. Augustine insisted, but so are critical reasoning, autonomous judgment, and presumption. And, what is often forgotten, the humans really do achieve something very significant in the eyes of their Creator: "Behold, the [hu]man *has become like one of us,* knowing good and evil. . . ."

The great paradox of the story is that what *we* regard as sources of human glory—freedom, critical reasoning, autonomous judgment, quasi-divine knowledge—become the sources of human shame. Self-consciousness, in its double sense of self-awareness and embarrassment, comes into being: "Then the eyes of both were opened, and they knew that they were naked." Whatever else the Genesis story may teach us, it at least teaches us this, that the sources of the most profound human miseries and failures are somehow bound up with the sources of the most glorious human achievements. This tragic dimension to human existence involves the failure of human beings to accept their common humanity. It is, in brief, the impious quest for knowledge.

For our purposes here, the most important point of the story is this: the pursuit of knowledge as power disrupts community and disorders the cosmos. Male domination, for example, arises in the story, not as a divine prescription for how human life ought to be lived, nor as a divine punishment for transgression. Rather, it is one of the several immediate consequences of *human* creation, of the kind of disorderly world that the woman and the man and the serpent have brought upon themselves. Gender conflict and inequality are a small part of a much larger pattern of disharmony that includes enmity between humans and other animals, a struggle between humans and the vegetable world, and the replacement of life by death. Male rule over females is not *sanctioned* by the Creator as a kind of recipe for order; instead, it is one of the several marks of disorder that characterize the cultural world (the world that the humans have made) as opposed to the divinely ordered world (the world as it emerged originally from the hands of its Creator).

Knowledge as power destroys community through an exceptionally subtle process. After they have eaten from the tree of knowledge, the humans first hide themselves from one another, fashioning aprons for themselves, before they then hide together from the Creator. Having tasted of divinity, securing the knowledge that they are and have always been exposed and vulnerable together, the woman and the man strive instantly to conceal that vulnerability. It is an endeavor that leads di-

rectly to estrangement between them. By the time that the Lord God
finds them out, they are already quarreling, accusing, distrusting. The
battle between the sexes takes place in the action of the story *before* the
Creator announces that it will become a part of human life.

The story thus charts in a very careful manner a movement from one
kind of loneliness to completed human community to disobedience to
loss of complete community to another kind of loneliness. This narrative
sequence, whose midpoint involves the aspiration to be divine, is
framed by two very different kinds of separation from the divine. In the
first instance, the *Lord God* observes that humanity is alone, solitary by
virtue of the distance between Creator and creature. In the second instance, the *humans* observe that they have estranged themselves from
the Creator, having already estranged themselves from each other and
having thus undone the divine remedy for the solitary condition of
original humanity.

Needless to say, the second state of separation is worse than the first.
Paradoxically worse—naturally. For the human aspiration to divinity
includes, among other things, the desire for autonomy and self-
sufficiency, a denial both of creatureliness and of the fundamental human need for community. But in becoming ''like God,'' the humans
discover *for themselves* that ''it is not good the human should be alone.''
Unfortunately, in the course of discovering this, the humans also become so fully aware of their vulnerability that they forever seek to
conceal it. And in seeking to conceal it, they fatally jeopardize the
possibility of that full community that their nakedness made possible,
even necessary, in the beginning.

Education in a Disordered World

The end of the story in Genesis 2–3 does suggest that human beings are
powerless by themselves to return to Eden. The human condition does
seem permanently flawed by the conflicts that mark both our inner and
outer, our psychological and our social, lives. Indeed, the conditions
described in Genesis 3 seem so fraught with difficulty that mortality
seems more a blessing than a curse. But if Genesis 3 diagnoses and
describes our present predicament, Genesis 2 remains the horizon of our
hopes. It is one thing to say that we are permanently flawed, quite
another to suggest that we should act to deepen and maintain those flaws
as though they were divinely ordained. And, of course, we do not act

this way for the most part. We do not suggest that we should *not* act to alleviate human suffering. Nor do we ordinarily argue that leisure is an evil, since we were meant to labor and struggle.

To some degree, higher learning *must* therefore include a range of research efforts for the relief of humanity's estate. And these worthy ambitions will surely involve, to some extent, the pursuit of knowledge as a form of power over disordered natural processes. Even so, if we are mindful of the teaching of Genesis, we can carry these enterprises responsibly forward if and only if they are advanced by human beings who are imbued with a sense of limits. This sense of limits will entail, as we have seen, a kind of piety. But it will also engage our natural capacity to live nobly in the midst of ambiguities and paradoxes of the kind that inform the Genesis story of our collective condition. Finally, this sense of limits will be less a moment of insight and more of a spiritual virtue cultivated by practices of teaching and learning that aspire to recreate the companionable community that was the first object of human thought.

III

All academics are exiles from Eden; indeed, all human beings are in this condition. None can escape the dialectics of Eden that, as we have seen, continue in the West to shape the aspirations and the fears of the religious and the nonreligious alike. Many of the successes of the technological project of mastery make us all feel less rather than more in control of our destinies. Moreover, a purely technological education fractures community, as it has apparently for most symbolic analysts, by obscuring the social dimensions of knowledge and by replacing the quest for truth with a quest for power. For some, the ensuing sense of chaos leads to desperate efforts, many of them artistic, to make the world all over again and so to control it totally through a kind of deliberate self-deception. Others resign themselves to a distinctively modern kind of permanent estrangement, marked by a tendency to regard the world as object and the self as an alien presence in but not of it. The modern research university, insofar as it gives itself over entirely to the project of *Wissenschaft,* of "mastering all things by calculation," allows itself to become the principal institutional agent of these dubious enterprises. Once having done so, the modern research university, forsaking *homo sapiens* for *homo faber,* cannot credibly claim to be pursuing the life of virtue.

The principal heresy of modernism, the one that animates the research university, is, like all heresies, not so much a falsehood as an obsessive exaggeration of one truth to the point of distortion. Clifford Geertz, in *Interpretation of Cultures,* identifies and then identifies himself with one source of this heresy, when he says that he believes, "with Max Weber, that man is an animal suspended in webs of significance he himself has spun. . . ."[2] The image here is uncanny, vindicating Adams's prescient sense that he was a kind of prototypical modern figure. As we saw, Adams characterized himself as "a spider [who] had to spin a new web in some new place with a new attachment." If we must think of ourselves as spiders spinning webs of meaning, we should be sure to reflect upon the less comforting features of this image: the thin fragility of our connections to the world.

The Weberian emphasis upon the making of meaning explains in part why cultural anthropology has become the latest in a long series of organized intellectual endeavors that have occupied, however temporarily, the position of queen of the academic disciplines. It bases this claim to supremacy not at all upon the prospect of synthesis, as theology and philosophy once did, but upon its wholly legitimate possession of the form of analysis best suited to modern pluralism—the semiotically informed interpretation of the myriad meanings that allegedly constitute human life as we know and live it.

However vital and important this endless task of interpretation might be, it cannot be the whole of education. If it is the whole, the whole is then a mere heap, an assemblage of cultural inventories and linguistic practices, and we must all agree with Henry Adams, who thought, after a time, that education was mere mastery of a certain set of tools such as languages and mathematics. We will come also to agree fully with Perry, who thinks of education as training in the making of meaning and yet who wonders why, given this understanding, the university should produce so many disaffected multiplists.

The critical commentary offered here does not promise a new intellectual synthesis, nor does it wish to deny either the facts of pluralism or the need for a profound acknowledgment of human creativity. Spiritually grounded education in and for thoughtfulness seeks the cultivation of those virtues that make the communal quest for the truth of matters possible, an undertaking that is in every sense prior to both the explication of various systems of meaning and the project of *Wissenschaft*. As we said earlier, this conception of higher learning insists both that religion needs Enlightenment and that Enlightenment needs religion.

IV

But matters are somewhat more complicated than this latter formula suggests. My selection of the creation story in Genesis and my particular reading of that story demonstrate that one cannot be ''religious in general,'' but that one must speak, as I have throughout this book, from a particular religious tradition. As it happens, that tradition tends to construe the world, including the part of it discussed here as ''higher education,'' as good *but* systemically flawed, as animated by a range of noble ideals and aspirations *but* unable fully to realize them, as simultaneously graced and disgraced. Moreover, the sense of vocation I have advanced here depends upon a sense of a cosmos that is not of our own making. A calling, in the full sense of the word, requires a call that comes to us from a source outside ourselves.

Though Genesis is sacred Scripture to me as a Christian, I offer my reading of it here, not as an antimodern tract, one that would correct Adams, Joyce, and Weber, by returning us to some original state of relative purity. Instead, I read it as, among other things, a cautionary tale about the powers and limits of human knowledge and human reason, one that should make us equally suspicious of the arrogance of modernity and of wholesale rejections of modernity in the name of some version or another of an educational fantasy. Because I worship a God who called His creation ''good'' and who, because He ''so loved the world,'' continues to redeem it through the actions of human beings in history, I cannot but love that small portion of the world I have been criticizing throughout this book, the modern research university.

This ambivalence, grounded equally in my religious convictions and in my own experience of the academy, has led me consistently to resist the more radical and dramatic educational remedies that are proposed, right and left, in contemporary discourse about the university. As I have tried to demonstrate, much that already takes place within the secular academy exemplifies what I have called education in and for thoughtfulncss. And the Enlightenment emphases upon disengaged reason, tolerance, and freedom of inquiry that are preserved and defended at the best universities have served as a powerful corrective to the sometimes violent effects of religious fanaticisms. On the other hand, the Weberian ethos still prevails, and that ethos does obscure the highest and best calling of the university itself: the spirited search for the truth of matters.

This kind of ambivalent appraisal is similar to and to some extent warranted by the story told by Charles Taylor that I alluded to previously. The problems of the research university as we have considered them here are the same problems Taylor attributes to modern culture as a whole. This should not surprise us, because the research university is perhaps the most characteristic institution of modernity, and as such it both manifests and to some degree perpetuates the dilemmas that collectively define the moral predicament of our times. Thus, to address thoughtfully and critically the *ethos* of the academy is to address, in a focused way, the deepest difficulties within contemporary culture.

Taylor closes his rich and comprehensive portrait of the modern identity with a set of worries similar to those that have haunted the foregoing discussion. He expresses them as a set of questions that are fitting as a conclusion here in that they serve as a guide to further inquiry:

> The question . . . is whether we are not living beyond our moral means in continuing allegiance to our standards of justice and benevolence. Do we have ways of seeing-good which are still credible to us, which are powerful enough to sustain those standards? If not, it would be more honest and more prudent to moderate them. . . . Is the naturalist seeing-good, which turns upon the rejection of the calumny of religion against nature, fundamentally parasitic? This it might be in two senses: not only that it derives its affirmation through an alleged negation, but also that the original model for its universal benevolence is *agape*. How well could it survive the demise of the religion it strives to abolish? With the "calumny" gone, could the affirmation continue?[3]

Those who are also troubled by these latter questions and who find themselves sympathetic to the redescriptions and remedies that the present book offers might turn to Taylor's work for further edification. Those who hold views at sharp variance with my own should consider whether, without the cultivation and sustenance of the virtues I have outlined here, subsequent debate about higher learning can possibly proceed without violence to the noble but fragile practices of inquiry that they and I would want in these times to preserve, renew, and transmit to the next generation.

Notes

1. Phyllis Trible, *God and the Rhetoric of Sexuality* (Fortress Press: Philadelphia, 1978), 80; Gould, "Freudian Slip, *Natural History* 96 (February, 1987), 16.

2. "Thick Description: Toward an Interpretive Theory of Culture," in Clifford Geertz, *The Interpretation of Cultures* (Basic Books: New York, 1973), 5.

3. Charles Taylor, *Sources of the Self: The Making of the Modern Identity* (Harvard University Press: Cambridge, 1989), 517.

Index

Academic vocation, three conceptions of, 5–6; and quest for meaning, 95; and friendship, 19, 61–63; and scholarship, 75–76; Henry Adams's conception of, 118–19; Max Weber's conception of, 6–16, 95, 102–109; religious reconception of, 22, 45, 58–63, 67, 84–88, 136

Adam, 96, 127–29

Adams, Charles Francis, 113

Adams, Charles Francis, Jr., 113, 122 n. 10

Adams, Henry, 110–18; and modern educated personality, 119; and multiplicity, 99–100; and St. Augustine, 96, 121–22; *Education of,* 102–10, 120–22

Apaideusia, 87–88

Apollo, 53, 57

Arendt, Hannah, 96–97

Aristotle, 19, 48, 62–63, 86–88

Arnold, Matthew, 27

Asceticism, Puritan, 13–14; Protestant worldly, 12, 118–19

Augustine, 45, 48, 57, 91, 100, 104, 111, 127, 132. *See also* Henry Adams

Bellah, Robert, 88, 111

Bernard of Clairvaux, 60

Bernstein, Richard, 28

Beruf, 6–7, 10, 12–15, 18, 57. *See also* Academic vocation

Berufsmensch, 10, 13–14

Bildung, 7–9, 16–18, 59, 122

Bloom, Allan, 85–87

Bok, Derek, and 1986–87 Report to Harvard Board of Overseers, 3–5, 8–9, 16, 18, 20 n. 1

Booth, Wayne, 18, 63

Bricolage, 40, 55–56

British University Grants Committee, 70

Brubaker, Rogers, 10

Calling. *See* Academic vocation

Calvin, John, 57; Calvinism, 14–17, 42 n. 19

Cameron, J. M., 70, 79

Campbell, Courtney, 76

Caritas, 10–11, 60. *See also* Charity

Character, formation of, 3–6, 13, 45, 56, 79, 85, 111–12, 122; Hume's qualities of, 46; of the community of learning, 35–37,

139

128, 133–35, 137. *See also* Charity, Faith, Humility, Piety, Self-sacrifice
Vocation. *See* Academic vocation

Waldron, Jeremy, 38
Weber, Max, and alienation, 16, 63; and asceticism, 14; and friendship, 44, 59, 61; and Henry Adams, 96, 100, 102, 109, 118, 122, 127; and Hume, 46; and means-end rationality, 38–39, 58; and rationalization, 9–10, 17; and

specialization, 13; and the academic calling, viii, 6–16, 78, 95, 122, 128; contemporary criticism of, 18–19
Whitehead, Alfred North, 31
William of Ockham, 45
Wissenschaft als Beruf, 6–7, 12–15, 57
Wissenschaft, 58–62, 92, 97
Wittgenstein, Ludwig, 24
Wolin, Sheldon, 13–14
Workshop in the History of the Human Sciences, 78